THE
POLITICAL PRIMER

Fundamentals of Politics

MARK E. GLOGOWSKI, Ph.D.

Order this book online at www.trafford.com
or email orders@trafford.com

Most Trafford titles are also available at major online book retailers.

© Copyright 2011 Mark E. Glogowski, Ph.D..
All rights reserved. No part of this publication may be reproduced, stored in a
retrieval system, or transmitted, in any form or by any means, electronic, mechanical,
photocopying, recording, or otherwise, without the written prior permission of the author.

Printed in the United States of America.

ISBN: 978-1-4669-0631-0 (sc)
ISBN: 978-1-4669-0630-3 (e)

Trafford rev. 02/22/2012

 www.trafford.com

North America & international
toll-free: 1 888 232 4444 (USA & Canada)
phone: 250 383 6864 ♦ fax: 812 355 4082

AUTHOR BIO

The author, Mark E. Glogowski PhD, earned a bachelor of science from the University of Rochester, a master of science from Rochester Institute of Technology, and a PhD from the University of Arizona. Living in upstate New York with his wife, Kathleen, he enjoys the company of two daughters, a son-in-law, and an energetic grandchild. With forty-seven years of research experience, and after having held leadership positions in several organizations, clubs, and committees, including serving as town leader for a political party, he considers himself to be a typical retired professional American.

Shortly after retiring, he ran in a primary for a town office against another candidate and came face-to-face with a problem that every candidate has to confront: the voting public's apathy and lack of knowledge and understanding of politics. He lost. This motivated the author to use a research approach to study this problem. His goal was to find a way to get individuals to quickly determine for themselves what they politically believe, then to correlate their beliefs to a political party's philosophy, and then to evaluate the candidates. Dr. Glogowski believes that with the proper tools, it would be possible for the voter to confidently choose a candidate that would represent the voter on every issue.

He found a set of tools and tested them. Having presented the tools to numerous adult education classes, the positive responses motivated him to write this political primer.

The author believes that, by the time you finish reading *The Political Primer,* you will understand politics and its purpose will be clear. You will never view politics the same again.

DEDICATED TO
KATHLEEN, KATRINA, AND MICHELLE

A NOTE FROM THE AUTHOR

This Political Primer provides you with essential basic political information that many politicians do not want you to know. Politicians do not want you to discover what it is that you believe, and they do not want you to fully understand politics. If they can keep you politically naive, and then get you to become involved in politics, they can make you their political pawn.

To most people today the following statements are political wisdom and political reality:

- This is how elected officials approach a controversial issue and how they decide which side of the issue they are going to support with their vote: They first determine the number of voters that support one side of the issue versus the other. Then they balance that information against the amount of money they can raise for their campaign coffers by supporting one side versus the other.
- This is what is often suggested to try when you are trying to decide who to vote for: Learn as much as you can about the issues being discussed and find out what each of the candidates say about those issues. Then identify the candidate that makes you angriest and vote for the other candidate.
- This is the suggested plan to implement when people inquire how to participate effectively in politics: Pick any issue that needs to be supported or to be changed. Then find people that believe the same way you do and begin demonstrating and writing letters. The more people you can get to demonstrate with you for the ideas you advocate, the more attention you will get from the elected officials. Eventually

an elected official will decide they want to get your group's support (i.e., votes) in the next election and they will listen to you.
- This is common voting strategy: Do not vote for the party: Vote for the individual.

That pretty much sums up the current political thought and advice to voters[1]. If these statements describe your current political beliefs and you consider these statements to be just common political wisdom that reflect the true nature of political Reality, then in reality you have been duped. You are probably also being used as a political pawn by politicians.

Politics is not about balancing issues supported by voters against issues supported by the campaign contributors. Politics is not about the issues at all. It is not about demonstrating just to get a politician's attention. Politics is not about gut feelings or emotions of any kind. The true objective of politics is to create and maintain the society you want to live in. To accomplish that goal you need to be involved. But, you first need to know what you believe about what should be. This Political Primer will help you clarify your beliefs

It is all about you. Politics is about you and what you want. Politics is not about the candidate, not about the party, not about the issues, and not about what other people believe[2]. Politics is about what you believe. But, what do you believe? If you want to know what you believe, you can not start by discussing candidates, issues, or what other people believe. The starting point to finding out what you believe is yourself. In this Political Primer, your starting point will be your answers to two Political Interrogatories. As you begin to understand how your answers to the Political Interrogatories form your political beliefs, you will begin to change the way you look at politics. Change in society – meaningful political change – will only begin when you grasp a clear understanding of what it is that you believe and why you believe it. Your political beliefs create your vision of the society that you want to live in.

The Political Interrogatories deal with two concepts that you have already grappled with as you became an adult. The two concepts, later referred to as Survival concepts, form the foundation of four, and only four political Worldviews. You have already pondered these concepts and as a result you have already chosen one of the four Worldviews as your political Worldview. The first goal of the Political Primer will be to discuss those two concepts, why they are important, and how they form the four Worldviews. You will then begin to recognize your conclusions regarding the two concepts and the Worldview you have already chosen. You will learn not only which Worldview you embraced, but as you proceed through this Political Primer, you will also learn why you embraced that Worldview.

Once you have grasped the significance of the four Worldviews, understand how the Worldviews are related to political beliefs, and recognize how those political beliefs create society, everything in the political arena will begin to come into sharp focus. Before you finish the Political Primer you may, perhaps for the first time, begin to see how all the pieces of the political picture fit together. If this is the first time everything begins to make sense, the sensation you will experience will be similar to the experience of seeing the three dimensional images in Magic Eye® pictures for the first time[3]. The right kind of 'political change' begins when you determine what kind of society you want to live in, and you then begin to utilize your Worldview to engineer solutions that will create that society.

Three facts about politics. This Political Primer is humbly offered as a way for you to re-discover, or discover for the first time, your political beliefs. You will soon realize politics is not about what other people think or what other people believe. Politics is about what you think and what you believe. Here are three of the facts that politicians and elected officials do not want you to know:

1. Politics is not complicated.
2. Only four basic political philosophies exist.
3. Politics is entirely about you!

THE PREMISE OF THE POLITICAL PRIMER

The basic premise of the Political Primer is as follows:

1) Everyone grapples with two fundamental concepts about life.
2) Those two concepts form four unique Worldviews.
3) Those Worldviews form the basis of all politics.
4) Every individual selects one Worldviews as their Worldview.
5) Your Worldview is the foundation of your political beliefs
6) Determining your Worldview is the first and most important step you can take to understand your political beliefs.
7) The Gap between your Worldview and the Reality you experience is your political Gap. It is the driving force of politics.
8) The Worldview of those individuals who are placed in positions of authority over society determines the structure of society.

HOW THE POLITICAL PRIMER IS STRUCTURED

Part 1 begins with a discussion of the two Survival concepts and a discussion of your perception of Reality. It is established right up front why politics is important – Politics is War! It is also established right up front whether you might have been politically bamboozled. The introduction of the Political Awareness Confusion Factor (PAC Factor) will create a baseline of your current political beliefs. You will be introduced to PU statements (Political Untruths) and you will learn how they are utilized to get you to support solutions for society's problems that are totally contrary to your Worldview goals. After introducing the fundamental political concepts, you will be presented with the Political Interrogatories. By the end of Part 1, you will understand what 'Worldviews' are, you will know which Worldview you have already chosen, and you will know everything you need to know to understand politics. Not only will you understand why you consider one Worldview right, you will know why you consider the other three Worldviews to be wrong and what causes you to hold that belief. You will understand the political goals of four major political parties in the United States, and you will have been introduced to four new political terms. Having been introduced to a completely new way of choosing a candidate, you will never again have to resort to your 'gut feeling' or to choosing the person that angered you the least. You will have confidence that the candidate you support with your vote will always represent you and your beliefs for as long as they are in office, and you will have confidence that they will do so on every issue.

Part 2 presents a variety of issues to illustrate the application of the fundamental political principles presented in Part 1. By the time you finish Part 2 you will have confirmed for yourself that politics is not complicated, that the four political philosophies identified in Part 1 are real and have meaning, that it is not the issue that is important but the Worldview held by you, and that the Worldview you have chosen to embrace is indeed the right Worldview. However, if you determine that you do not want to live in the society that the Worldview you currently hold will create, by the time you finish Part 2 you will have chosen a different Worldview.

Part 3 contains essays concerning Moderates, Party Jumpers, and Judges. These essays will illustrate the richness of the perspective gained by applying the principles taught in Part 1. Another essay, "Changing the Country for the Worst with One Catchy Slogan" will confirm the power of this new perspective. The essay 'Interrelationship of Concepts" will review and further clarify the concepts that were introduced and used throughout the Primer. The final essay will revisit the immigration issue and will illustrate the power of Worldviews. This essay will provide an explanation of the impact Worldviews have on society, completing the political picture of how Worldviews create the structure of society, and how a Worldview's structure of society changes society as solutions are implemented that are consistent with that Worldview. That is the true goal of politics.

Epilog. By the time you reach the Epilog you will have fully developed and embraced your Worldview. The bias in the Epilog reflects the Worldview that the author embraces. You may agree or disagree with the comments presented. Knowing why you agree or disagree with those comments is the goal of this Political Primer. The Epilog is the final test. If you hold a different Worldview you will believe the ideas and structure proposed for society as elaborated on in the Epilog are wrong. If you hold the same Worldview as the author, you will agree with the author's comments in the Epilog and will believe every concept presented concerning the structure of society is what should be. There should be no middle ground. Most importantly, regardless of whether you believe the ideas presented in the Epilog are right or wrong, if the Political Primer achieved its intended goal, you will know why you believe the ideas in the epilog to be right or wrong. And, because you will understand the foundation upon which you base your beliefs, you will know what must change to create a world consistent with your Worldview. When you know why you agree or disagree, you will have indeed become politically astute.

Appendix A. This appendix presents a short discussion of the issue of gender – or the lack thereof in the text, and how this author chose to avoid the "he/she" grammatical constructions by the use of a common verbal practice.

Appendix B. For those that believe politics is just too complicated to be boiled down into four basic political philosophies, that the approach to politics presented in Part 1 is too simplistic to be valid, and that politics today is rife with people deliberately spreading unbridled confusion, be assured that if you let it, politics can very quickly become very complicated. The cause of the confusion in politics is discussed in Part 1. The essay in Appendix B, "Complicating politics – how easily it occurs", illustrates mathematically how quickly politics can become very confusing and complicated because of a lack of understanding of the basics.

Glossary. Frequently used terms are defined.

CONTENTS

Author Bio v
A Note From The Author ix
The Premise Of The Political Primer xiii
How The Political Primer Is Structured xv

PART ONE
THE FUNDAMENTALS OF POLITICS

Chapter 1
    Politics – It Is All About You 3

Chapter 2
    Six Fundamental Political Concepts 5

Chapter 3
    Politics is War! 13
    Things To Think About 24

Chapter 4
    Reflect on Yourself 25

Chapter 5
    The Political Interrogatories. 39

Chapter 6
    Four Political Philosophies 53

Chapter 7
    Four New Political Terms 61

Chapter 8
    That's It! 73

PART TWO
APPLICATION OF THE FOUR WORLDVIEWS

Something To Think About 78

Chapter 9
Introduction to the Application of Worldviews 79

Chapter 10
Your Reality – Your Worldview 81

Chapter 11
Creating the Structure of Society 85

Chapter 12
Health Care 91

Chapter 13
The Homeless 97

Chapter 14
Lifeguards on a Pristine Beach 101

Chapter 15
The Use of Cushioned Lawn Furniture 105

Chapter 16
Use of Deadly Force by Private Citizens 109
Something to Think About 112

Chapter 17
The Worldview of Judges 113

Chapter 18
Abortion 121

Chapter 19
Support for the Fetus/Child. 131

Chapter 20
Illegal Immigrants. 135

Chapter 21
Implementing An Advocate's Solution to
Illegal Immigration 139

Chapter 22
    The Future Societies of Each of the Four Worldviews..... 147

Chapter 23
    The Worldview Future Political Roles of the Individual.. 149

Chapter 24
    The Ultimate Society. 151

PART 3
THE IMPACT OF WORLDVIEWS

    Something to think about 166

Chapter 25
    Introduction to Part 3 167

Chapter 26
    The Moderate... 169

Chapter 27
    Beware the Party Jumpers 173

Chapter 28
    Changing the Country for the Worst with
    One Catchy Slogan 177

Chapter 29
    Judges 181

Chapter 30
    Interrelationship of Concepts 191

Chapter 31
    Immigration – Illegal Immigration 201

Chapter 32
    Final Comment 215

EPILOG

What is Mightier than the Pen 217
Appendix A
    The He/She Dilemma 237
Appendix B
    Politics Can Become Very Complex Very Quickly 239

Glossary 253
Endnotes 257

PART ONE

THE FUNDAMENTALS OF POLITICS

Politics begins with you.
Politics is about what you believe.
If you know what you believe and why –
politics is not that complicated.

CHAPTER 1

POLITICS – IT IS ALL ABOUT YOU

Is it any wonder that most Americans are mystified and bewildered when it comes to politics? Political rhetoric and dribble spews forth every day – from candidates, from their supporters, from group leaders, from demonstrators, from talk show hosts, from pulpits, from ordinary citizens. A constant barrage of ideas and propaganda with conflicting opinions, fears, facts, claims, accusations, charges, distortions, ... and on and on .... from newspapers, campaign literature, flyers, magazines, books, movies, documentaries, infomercials, emails, websites, blogs, facebooks, twitters, youtubes – an avalanche inundating the average citizen with more information than can be digested in a hundred lifetimes.

You try to make sense of it all, but who is right? A thunderous roar of political emotions and convictions seems to be hemorrhaging from society. You are stymied. How do you sort through all the facts? How do you make sense of it all? Then, all of a sudden, you hear a comment and instantly you agree. "Yes. That's the way it should be!" Finally! A glimmer of what you believe about how society should work. As you try to build on the revelation, the vision disappears. Was it real or was it a mirage? All that remains are questions. Why did you agree? Why did you disagree? What is the foundation upon which you were building your political opinion? Deep down in your gut you know there must be some concepts that form the foundation of political beliefs. But what are they?

If politics is to change in a meaningful way, voters need to learn the fundamental political concepts and how they interrelate. They then need to determine from the fundamental concepts what it is that they themself[1] each believe about politics. Politics will not be meaningful to you until you understand the foundation upon which you base your political opinion and exactly what it is that you yourself believe and why you believe it.

You are the Center of the Political Universe. Every politician worth their weight in salt knows that politics is about what you want and what you believe. The entire focus of politics is on you. How do you want society to develop? How do you want people to interact? What kind of world do you want to live in? "What is it that you believe?" If you can not clearly and distinctly answer these questions you are in a political fog. Everything political that you observe will reflect your fog of uncertainty.

You will soon discover your political beliefs, starting with the concepts from which your political beliefs are derived.

He who knows others is wise.
He who knows himself is enlightened.

–Lao-tzu

CHAPTER 2

SIX FUNDAMENTAL POLITICAL CONCEPTS

You can participate in politics as a voter or as a candidate without ever knowing what the fundamental political concepts are. But, if you are unaware of what the fundamental political concepts are, will you ever really understand politics?

There are six concepts that define politics. They are reviewed in this chapter. They are: "Expectation" and "Responsibility", "Reality" and "Worldviews", and "Good" and "Evil". While you may have just shuddered to think that you are going to be subjected to a long winded, dry, mind-numbing discourse about concepts you could care less about – relax. You have already given these concepts much thought and you deal with them every day. You just never gave the concepts names. [Besides, the pain will be over before you know it.]

Survival Concepts. Expectation deals with nothing more than your prediction of how a pending interaction with another person is going to turn out. Is the interaction going to be pleasant, good, and desirable? Or, do you expect it to be bad, horrendous, and undesirable? Responsibility deals with nothing more than your opinion of whether you want to have the authority to make decisions on matters that affect you and whether you believe you should have the authority to make those decisions.

That's pretty simple and straight forward, isn't it? Your experience has taught you that before and during every interaction with other people you must establish an Expectation concerning the outcome of the interaction and you need determine who is going to be Responsible during the interaction to make any necessary decisions. In some situations your very survival may depend on your snap decisions on these two matters.

The two concepts, Expectation and Responsibility, are fundamental Survival concepts. The other four concepts listed are derived from these two concepts.

I'm OK. You're OK. The two Survival concepts, Expectation and Responsibility, are the subject matter of a 1969 book written by Thomas A. Harris, M.D., I'm OK. You're OK[5]. He stated that each person, as they matured, developed Expectations and created a personal concept of Responsibility. According to Dr. Harris, you arrived at your opinion through a series of subconscious events. He characterized these events as internal interactions that occur between the individual's three 'subconscious alter egos'. He referred to the alter egos as the "Parent', the "Child", and the "Adult". The average person would refer to these subconscious internal interactions of the Parent, Child, and Adult alter egos as nothing more than their having agonized over what they experienced and agonized about what they should do next. Nevertheless, Dr Harris stated that every member of society struggles with these two Survival concepts and ultimately everyone adopted one of the following views as their concept of Reality.

"I am OK, you are OK"
"I am OK, you are not OK"
"I am not OK, you are OK"
"I am not OK, you are not OK"

Right now, it probably is not difficult for you to look at those four short phrases and conclude that one is consistent with what you believe and the other three statements do not reflect Reality as you perceive it to be.

NOTE TO READER: Consciously, right now, take the time and determine which expression best represents your view of Reality.

The statement you selected is your Reality. At any time you can select a different Reality, but you probably will not do so without a lot of agonizing. That is because the Reality you chose is Reality as you know it to be. Any experience you had that appeared to be an exception to your Reality you took with 'a grain of salt'. You took it as an exception to Reality. It will take a lot of grains of salt before you will ever consider changing your view of Reality. But according to Dr Harris, a dramatic conflict between your chosen Reality and your experience will cause your "Adult" alter ego to force you to consciously reconsider your conclusions concerning Reality.

The Impact of Your Reality . . . Dr. Harris stated that your choice of Reality is a reflection  of your belief concerning you and other people being basically Good or basically Evil. The consequence of your belief concerning people being basically Good or basically Evil is significant.

I'm OK (Basically Good) vs. I'm Not OK (Basically Evil). If, as you grew up, you made decisions that had good outcomes, you would have concluded that you are OK to make decisions. As a result you also concluded you are basically a Good person. Your willingness to assume Responsibility to make decisions for yourself and for others when necessary is a result of this favorable opinion of yourself.

If your decisions in the past resulted in so much anguish for yourself and for others that you concluded that any decision you make will be a bad decision, you will not want to make decisions. You will consider yourself to be incapable of making good decisions. Your experience has confirmed the fact that you are incapable of making good decisions. You are not OK. Whether you consider yourself to be OK or not OK to be Responsible to make decisions will, over time, lead you to conclude that you are basically Good – or basically Evil.

Being Good or Evil is not a decision, it is a conclusion . . . The concept of Expectation is a Survival concept that you use repeatedly and  automatically. Your Expectation of your ability to make decisions that do not produce undesired consequences creates your conclusion concerning whether you are Good or Evil. The Expectation you created of other people taking into consideration your needs and desires when they make decisions does not impact your conclusion concerning yourself being Good or Evil. Your Reality concerning yourself is the conclusion you drew from your experiences making decisions. The Expectation you created concerning whether other people will take into consideration your needs and desires resulted in your conclusion concerning whether you consider other people to be Good or Evil.

The Life Sequence Process. If you looked for the process you went through to come to the conclusions of whether you and other people were OK or not OK, you would have found a repetitious process with a sequence illustrated as follows:

1. Someone makes a decision.
2. Someone acts on that decision.
3. The action creates a consequence.
4. You evaluate the consequence.
5. You receive feedback concerning the consequence.
6. You then determine the desirability or undesirability of the consequence and the feedback.
7. You reflected on who made the decision.
8. The process then repeats itself.

This 'Life Sequence' occurs continuously, yet for the most part it is so automatic you are unaware that the Life Sequence occurs at all. The consequence and the feedback you receive from the Life Sequence reflects back onto the person that made the decision, not the person that acted and created the consequence of the decision. The person that acts and that is directly responsible for the consequence of a decision is usually irrelevant in the feedback. Only the person that made the decision is important.

So, as you grew up and made decisions you experienced consequences, received feedback concerning those decisions, and determined that you made good and wise decisions or you determined you made terribly foolish and bad decisions. After numerous episodes you concluded you are Good and OK to make decisions, or you concluded that you are Evil and not OK to make decisions. That conclusion is your concept of Responsibility.

At the beginning of the Life Sequence, what other people hold as their concept of Responsibility is irrelevant to you. At the start of every Life Sequence, it is your belief concerning whether you consider yourself to be OK or not OK to make good decisions that impacts your willingness to assume Responsibility to make the decisions. Your willingness or unwillingness to make decisions determines the Direction you will take. Your concept of Responsibility determines who will make the decision.

The second step in the Life Sequence is someone acting on the decision that you or someone else made. The Expectation you create concerning the pending interactions is dependant upon how you view other people: Are other people OK or not OK when they decide to act – regardless of who made the decision: Are people basically Good or are they basically Evil? Your Expectations reflect your experience, and your conclusions reflect the input you received from past Life Sequences. This is Reality – Your Reality!

Four basic Realities. There are four possible Realities according to Harris. Here is how they play out.

I'm OK – You're OK. If you have no concern about other people making decisions about matters that will impact you and if your Expectation is that other people will accommodate your concerns and needs when they make decisions, you consider other people to be OK. They are basically Good. Never-the-less, while you have no concern regarding other people making decisions, you also consider yourself to be OK. Your preference will be to make the decisions yourself.

I'm Not OK – You're OK. If your experiences have led you to believe other people are OK, basically Good people, and you consider yourself to be Not OK, basically Evil, your preference will be to defer to others to make decisions. Your Expectation is that other people will take your concerns and desires into account when they make the decisions. There is no need for you to be Responsible to make the decisions. Besides, in your mind, you and everyone else would be better off if other people made the decisions.

I'm OK – You're Not OK. If you believe other people are Not OK and basically Evil and believe yourself to be OK and basically Good, not only will you desire to make your own decisions but you will insist on making your own decisions! You will be adamant that any decisions made by other people be limited and restricted in scope. Why? Because your Expectation is that other people will not consider your needs or desires and they will make decisions that are harmful to you, to other people, and to themself.

I'm Not OK – You're Not OK. If you believe other people are basically Evil and you consider yourself to be basically Evil, you have a dilemma. You do not want to make decisions, but your experience taught you to establish the Expectation that other people will not take your needs, concerns, or desires into consideration. Other people are not OK. They are Evil. They only look out for themself. They will only consider their own wants and desires. If they make decisions, harm will come to you. So, while you may not want to be Responsible to make decisions, you clearly do not want other people to make decisions. You may not be able to make good decisions, but your preference is to make the decisions anyway and stack the consequences in your favor.[6]

So what does this have to do with politics? The two fundamental Survival concepts of Expectation and Responsibility are the foundation upon which you created your Reality. They are also the foundation upon which you created your Worldview.

Reality and Worldview . . .
If you ask yourself the right questions concerning the Survival  concepts you will determine for yourself what you believe about how the world does work. What you believe about how the world does work is your **Reality**.

If you consider the same concepts using a different set of criteria you will determine how you believe the world should work. What you believe about how the world should work is your **Worldview**.

Your Reality and your Worldview form your political beliefs. If your Reality and your Worldview differ, that difference is referred to as the political Gap. That Gap will create the potential and the motivation for you to become politically active.

The two Survival concepts formed four possible Realities. The same two concepts generate four Worldviews. Whether you are determining your Reality or your Worldview depends upon what you use to establish your conclusions. Your Reality is determined exclusively and entirely by your experiences. That is how the world works. That's Reality. You can perceive it no other way. Your Worldview however is determined by your experiences modified by your background – your education, training, upbringing, culture, religion, everything – even what you do and read for recreation. If you consider your experience and everything you learned about what was, what is, and what could be, you create your Worldview; you create a vision of how the world could and should work.

What is Practical – What is Right. Here is how you use the concepts of Reality and Worldview. You use your Reality concerning how the world <u>does</u> work as your guide to make decisions concerning what is practical and what is not practical. You use your Worldview concerning how the world <u>should</u> work to determine the rightness or wrongness of every solution to every personal and societal problem – regardless of whether the solution is practical or not.

The Gap is Not Static. The Gap between your Reality and your Worldview is what will motivate you to get into politics. That Gap – the Political Gap – drives politics. If the Gap becomes large enough you will say to

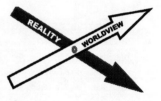

yourself, 'This just should not be.' You will want to close the Gap and that desire will motivate you to get involved in politics. Since politics is the process of solving problems, resolving issues, and establishing changes in the way people and governments interact, politics is always about change. But the focus of that change, the goal of politics, will be to close the Gap and make Reality as you perceive it to be, agree with your Worldview of how the world should work.

When the world <u>is</u> as it <u>should be</u>, there is no Gap between your Reality and your Worldview. Having no Gap can create a problem. With your Reality and your Worldview in complete harmony, the role of politics is easily forgotten and ignored. Without the motivating force of a Gap, there is no reason to exert energy to make your Reality and your Worldview consistent. They already are.

Unfortunately, the absence of a Gap is an unstable condition. There are two reasons a Gap will reappear.

The first reason is you. You can cause the Gap to reappear by actively seeking new experiences and new knowledge. If your new experiences change your Expectation or your concept of Responsibility, the new experiences will change your Reality. Those new experiences may not simultaneously change your Worldview. If your Reality changes and your Worldview does not change, that will cause a political Gap to appear. Alternatively, if new knowledge of what 'could be' means that the world could be better, your Expectations, or your concept of Responsibility, or both could change, and that could change your Worldview. Your Reality will not change because of what you learned, but if your new knowledge causes you to believe the world should work differently than the way it does work, then a political Gap will appear.

The second reason the Gap may appear is your complacency. When there is no Gap between your Reality and your Worldview, the world <u>is</u> as the world <u>should be</u>. You will be politically inactive. There is no Gap to close. Thus, there is no incentive to be involved. Unfortunately, as the Gap closes for you it widens for those individuals that hold a different Worldview. They become highly motivated. If they are politically successful they will change society to reflect their Worldview. When that happens, you will once again experience a political Gap because their changes will cause your experiences in Reality to become something that 'just should not be.

Politics is a vicious cycle, driven by the political Gap, and the individuals with the largest political Gap are always the most motivated to be involved in politics.

Building Your Foundation. These six concepts, Expectation, Responsibility, Good, Evil, Worldviews, and Reality are the critical political concepts used to build political philosophies and political beliefs.

CHAPTER 3

POLITICS IS WAR!

Politics is not a game. The goal of politics is to create a society where people interact the way that you believe that people should interact. That will only happen if and when individuals selected for public office share your Worldview. The process of selecting the leaders that will determine how society will function is referred to as politics. How serious is politics? <u>Politics is War</u>!

Control Over the Structure of Society. The objective in politics is to gain control over the structure of society in order to preserve it or to change it. War has the same objective – to gain control over the structure of society in order to preserve the current structure or to change it. Politics? War? The objective is the same.

The Method of Combat. The tactics and implements of political combat are radically different from physical combat, but they are just as effective. In war you create an army, supply it with weapons, and command it to fight your opponents, who are individuals that advocate a Worldview different from yours. You fight by killing your opponents. You win by surviving and being dominant on the battlefield: The benefit you get if you win is that you control the structure of society. In politics you find individuals that share your Worldview and you create a political party. You then select candidates to run for public office. You charge them to do battle with your opponents, who are individuals that advocate a Worldview different from yours. You fight by getting others to stand up and be counted as supporters of yours. You win by having the greater number of people stand up to be counted with you. Having the majority of the people stand with you will make you dominant on the political battlefield. The benefit you get if you win is that you control the structure of society. Perhaps this is why so many politicians and candidates claim they want to join the battle and 'fight' for you, why political parties refer to their headquarters as their command center, and why talk show hosts like "Quinn and Rose" refer to their broadcast as coming from the "war room"[7].

Your Job. As a member of the electorate, your job in the political battle is just to stand up and be counted: Thus the phrase,

They also serve who only stand up to be counted.

But there is the rub. In a democracy you get one chance to be counted (except for those committing election fraud). To be effective, you need to be counted with people of like mind to you. Where do you stand? Who are you being counted with? Who are you empowering to determine the structure of society? The stakes for you and society are high. You are at risk: In both politics and war you are the target.

A Deeper Understanding. In war, you are generally on one side by circumstance and you remain on that side to protect family and friends. When you are presented with information that creates an understanding of your side's cause, you would naturally increase your resolve and your support for your side's cause. However, if sufficient information is presented to create a still deeper understanding of the issues on both sides, and if you begin to believe your side's cause was unjust and that the other side's cause was just, then and only then would you consider changing sides.

Who are you being counted with? For most people, choosing sides in politics is not much different than choosing sides in a war. The side you are on in war is usually a result of circumstances that have nothing to do with the cause of war. For the most part, the same is true in politics. In all likelihood, if you joined a political party you did so for trivial reasons.

Are you in the right party? Does it matter?

* If the party you joined was chosen arbitrarily because you didn't know what your Worldview was,
* if you still don't know what your Worldview is,
* if you don't understand how to formulate or recognize solutions consistent with your Worldview,

* if you don't know how to recognize the structural changes in society that are caused by the solutions proposed by others,
* if you can not determine how the structure of society will change when those you support get into office,

then do you even care who you are being counted with? Does it matter?

Candidates, campaign managers, and supporters of candidates will gladly provide you with hundreds of reasons why it does not matter and why it is not possible to determine a candidate's Worldview. What is their motivation for doing so? Simple. Politics is war. If you can be duped into believing that you can't determine another person's Worldview or that it doesn't matter, then even if you could determine a candidate's Worldview, maybe you won't try. That would make their job a lot easier.

There are two good reasons why you should try to determine what a politician's Worldview is: First, because you can! Second, because that is the only way you will know for sure whether the politician will truly represent you and pursue your Worldview after they take office.

A Politician's Job Half Done. While the focus of this Political Primer is on your Worldview, keep in mind that everyone has developed their Worldview just as you have developed your Worldview. Every individual, whether voter, bureaucrat, politician, elected official, dictator, or king, has consciously or subconsciously adopted one of the four Worldviews as their own. Their chosen Worldview is their compass and guide when making decisions. The type of world that people in power are attempting to create is determined by their Worldview, not yours. The politician's job, when seeking your support in an election, is to convince you that you and the politician share the same Worldview, that both of you share the same goals, and that the politician will make the same decisions you would make if you were in office. If you understand that the politicians' goal is to convince you that you share the same Worldview, then it is easy to understand why politics is not about what the politicians say they want to do. Politics is about what you believe and it is about convincing you that the politician's beliefs and what the politician wants to do is consistent with your beliefs and is exactly what you want to have done. The politician is counting on you to not know what you believe. That way the politician's job is half done. Now all they have to do is to manipulate you into voting for them. And, they have ways to do that!

Politics is War. Just as surely as the outcome of any war gives one group control over another group, our society's political, non-violent, democratic election process places individuals in positions of authority over society. With society's structure at stake, many politicians feel justified using any means necessary to win. If they win, they can be the ones to create society's structure and that structure will be based on their Worldview. Good political candidates will tell you that your Worldview, what you believe about how society should work, is important. But, if the politician holds to a different Worldview, your Worldview is not important to them. In their effort to win, many politicians will do everything and anything they can to get you to believe that they share your beliefs, except tell you what their Worldview is. They will do everything and anything they can to control what you think you believe. *Remember: Politics is War.* To the extent that they can get you to accept a statement such as "Politics really doesn't matter that much." – then they win! If they can get you to believe that you don't need to vote, that you don't need to be counted, that you are just one vote amongst millions, that you can't really make a difference – then hey! So much the better for them! That is just one less supporter of the other side. From the politician's perspective, if duplicity works, use it. To the extent that they can get you to agree to not talk politics and just talk about implementing a solution – which they have created – they win. You lose.

Political Ammunition. Most political candidates today have found that they do not have to share your political views to get your support. Using PU statements, "for the sake of society" pleas, feigned offense, and feigned injury to elicit your sympathy[8], as quickly as a magician's slight of hand, politicians can get you to set aside your Worldview. [*NOTE TO READER: PU statements* *are Politically Untrue statements and Politically Unrelated statements. PU statements are discussed later in this chapter and are the subject of Chapter 4]*

If those techniques prove ineffective, politicians have learned others. For instance, you can be manipulated when you are emotional, confused, or deprived of the facts. With modern communication vehicles, politicians are frequently choosing the emotional route: The more emotional the voter, the easier it is to manipulate that voter. Politicians use emotions of fear, anger, hostility, nationality, religious convictions, loyalty to a cause, "the children", confusion in turbulent times, for the sake of the community – the list is endless; all tools to get people to suppress their Worldview and ignore the politician's Worldview.

Another tactic often used is the recitation of a mantra[9] such as, "I am concerned about THE PROBLEM. Politicians like to be associated with problems. Not just any problem, but THE PROBLEM – the problem that drags along a lot of emotional baggage. Politicians know that when voters are emotional, the mere reference to THE PROBLEM will stir sufficient emotions in the electorate to gain votes. Politicians who stress THE PROBLEM hope that you the voter will never look deeper into the solutions they intend to implement. Politicians do not want you to logically reflect on the problem because the source of the problem is the conflict that exists <u>in you</u>, between your view of Reality and your Worldview of what should be. The conflict that exists between your concept of Reality and your Worldview is what motivates you to become politically active. The politician's entire support from you may depend upon their keeping the conflict alive. They don't want you to reflect on their solution because that would cause you to ask, 'how should society work?' If you ask that question you might determine that the candidate does not share your Worldview and that conclusion could cause you to begin supporting a different candidate. Politicians want THE PROBLEM to motivate you to engage in politics. They want the emotional baggage of THE PROBLEM to impair your ability to decide what you truly want done. Politicians don't want you to compare your Worldview against their Worldview. That is why politicians rarely provide details concerning their proposed solutions to THE PROBLEM: If voters compare Worldviews, some politicians would lose votes. For a politician, having sufficient problems with emotional baggage to reference during a campaign is similar to an army having sufficient ammunition during a battle: You don't want to run out of ammunition before the battle is over or you will lose soldiers . . . your army will lose the battle.

The Political Armored Tank. It is naive and dangerous to believe that it doesn't matter which Worldview is used as a guide to construct the solution to THE PROBLEM. Politicians use solutions to change society and they look for issues that have the greatest emotional response in people so they can manipulate the voters. Politicians will lob issue after issue at people, and when they see one that gets the response they desire they begin to modify their tactics to become affiliated with the issue and with the issue's "concerned citizens".

Concerned citizens! These are individuals so closely affiliated with an issue that they become politically naïve; so emotional that they will support anyone that states that their issue is of paramount importance; so trusting that they will never question the Worldview of one of their candidates. After all, their candidate shares their concern about THE PROBLEM. Concerned citizens almost never determine whether their candidate's priority is to pursue or to prevent the implementation of the solution the concerned citizens truly desire. They only hear that the candidate is concerned.

The concerned citizens are the armored tank of politics that politicians attempt to ride to victory. Powered by emotions, these groups campaign against people they consider opponents regardless of Worldviews. Politicians know that regardless of the issue the political tank is pursuing, the fate of society's structure is dependant upon the implementation of a solution – any issue will do. Politicians will ride these political tanks because they know they can create requirements for the implementation of a solution to any problem using their Worldview and those requirements will cause society to be restructured to conform to their Worldview: It doesn't even matter if the solution makes THE PROBLEM worse. Politicians want to win and they will jump on any political tank to do so. Any issue will do! The naïve concerned citizens will propel it

The Political Hand Grenade. Since the late 1960's, the political parties have become increasingly reluctant to discuss their core philosophical beliefs. The result has been the creation of political chaos. Today, many of the leaders of political parties don't even acknowledge their party has core beliefs. They freely endorse candidates who have embraced political philosophies contrary to the party's traditional Worldview ideals and philosophy, even to the point where candidates are chosen by party committees based exclusively upon how the candidate is perceived as being a vote getter[10]. To confuse matters even more for the electorate, candidates from one political party are endorsed by elected officials of opposing parties, and candidates are crossed-endorsed by parties where the cross-endorsements defy logic, such as candidates cross-endorsed by both the Liberal and Conservative parties, or by both the Democratic and Republican parties.

In the 2009 local elections, and again in the 2010 general elections, and again in the local elections of 2011, most of the candidates in the author's voting area did not even affiliate themselves with a political party in their campaign literature, and it was impossible to identify party affiliation of candidates on the lawn signs. Why did the candidates not want to be associated with the other party candidates? Did the candidate not want to be associated with the political party because they themself did not share the party's Worldview? Was it because the terms Liberal and Conservative have been blended into a mentality of 'the good us' versus 'the evil them' where 'the good us' is dependent upon the individual speaking, and 'the evil them' is the other group? Was it because of negative, anti political party label rhetoric? For whatever reason, it is clear that this deliberately perpetrated animosity and confusion by talk show hosts has created an environment where it has become not only acceptable, but expected that candidates will not freely disclose their political party affiliation. In this environment party leaders often nominate candidates that embrace Worldviews other than the party's Worldview – politically hostile candidates. Many of those candidates could never survive a primary. Never-the-less, they are vehemently defended by party leaders – who make every effort to block primaries.

This is the environment where the political hand grenade finds its intended target. The political hand grenade is the Politically Unrelated comment or Political Untruth: The PU statement. They are perpetrated to befuddle the party's membership and the electorate! The PU statements are provided as justification for nominating and supporting politically hostile individuals. PU statements include such statements as:

"It doesn't matter what the candidate's political beliefs are, this candidate is concerned about THE PROBLEM"

"This candidate is a good vote getter"

"The candidate has been a dedicated worker and deserves a chance"

"The candidate is well qualified".

You have heard them. They are political hand grenades. When PU statements are successfully used, unworthy candidates are nominated, long time party members bite their tongue and grind their teeth, and new party members question their party affiliation. The PU statements, like hand grenades, cause chaos and death by creating confusion and uncertainty in the electorate. When successful, PU statements will kill the political chances of any worthy candidate that may not have had as much experience, regardless of the fact that the candidate is more philosophically aligned with the party members.

The Political Assassin. Have you ever tried to discuss with another voter the philosophical political beliefs of a candidate. If you have, you were probably met very quickly with resistance and hostility:

"How do you know what the candidate believes? Are you a mind reader?"

"It doesn't matter what their political philosophy is. It is the candidate's stand on the issues that is important. Our candidate is concerned about _____."

"Your candidate is not worthy of support because they are not concerned about _____. They are only concerned about _____."

Fill in the blanks – the issues are irrelevant. Those comments are assassins that kill any rational attempt to discuss a candidate's worthiness to be the party's chosen candidate based on the Worldview held by the party and the individual.

The Political Pawns. Political parties are formed to gather together people that share the same Worldview. The purpose of the party is to choose candidates and party leaders that will work to create a society shaped by the group's shared Worldview. For every political party, the first qualifying requirement for the party's endorsement should be that the candidate embraces the party's Worldview. To remove that requirement defeats the purpose of the existence of the political party. The use of PU statements, such as "The candidate is highly qualified" or "The candidate is well funded" or 'for the sake of society' pleas, are all intended to prevent like-minded people from supporting a candidate that actually shares their Worldview. As political party leaders ignore and abandon the party's chosen Worldview, people leave the political parties. Their only recourse in the election is to vote for the individual, not the party.

As party members leave their party out of frustration, they leave behind a political base of politically naive individuals, upon which the party leaders become increasing dependant. Those naive individuals are identified in the next chapter by the PAC Factor test as political Victims, Stoolies, and Stookies. They are easily made the Pawns in politics. They are motivated and kept in check with PU statements – which they repeat as mantras to all they encounter. As the exodus of the politically astute continues, party leaders meet less and less resistance from the membership. They are unchallenged when they use their power to thwart the party's political purpose and promote candidates that do not adhere to the party's Worldview. They get away with their abuse of power because the membership ranks of the political parties are increasingly politically naive. The leaders quickly state that regardless of Worldview beliefs of the party or the incumbent, the incumbents are people with too much experience in the political arena to not be supported by the party.

Whether any of the candidates being promoted by the Pawns actually embrace the Worldview of the party is irrelevant to the

Pawns. The Pawns not only do not know what their Worldview is, they do not know what their party's Worldview is, and they do not have a clue as to how to determine the Worldview of the candidate. Without this knowledge, how are they going to independently determine who to support?

So! The politically naïve Pawns push the party's chosen candidates. Big deal. If you don't know what your Worldview is, and if you don't really know what your party's Worldview is, and if you can't determine what the candidate's Worldview is, then why would those candidates being pushed by the political party's Pawns not be just as good a choice for you as any other candidate you might choose?

The naïve, easily manipulated political Pawns are a source of political power as they lob a barrage of PU statement hand grenades at the electorate. With the help of the Pawns, eventually, everyone's Worldviews will be ignored.

The Roadside Bomb. At one extreme, political Pawns blindly support incumbents. At the other extreme, to counter the political Pawns, are the politically naïve that want to vote every incumbent out of office. After all, all politicians are crooks. [Note that "All politicians are crooks" is a PU Statement] Why discriminate? Change for the sake of change! The logic behind the PU statement 'all politicians are crooks' is that the PU statement justifies the campaign of 'change for the sake of change'. This approach to politics is like fighting a war where you shoot everyone seen carrying a weapon regardless of whose side they are on. You place roadside bombs to blow up everyone that comes down the road no matter who they are. The statement 'All politicians are crooks.' is equivalent to the statement, "Everyone involved in fighting a war is hostile." If you remove everyone with a weapon, problem solved, the war is over.

The Foot Soldier. You are the foot soldier in politics. An increasing number of voters are calling for change for the sake of change. An increasing number of other voters are being duped into believing politics doesn't matter and they are openly declaring that they will not vote. Still others are claiming they will cross party lines when they vote because they recognize the dishonesty of the party leaders when they nominate and support

The Political Primer

certain candidates. One can only wonder – what is going on with the American electorate and in the American political parties. Voting for a candidate 'across party lines' would mean either you or the candidate is in the wrong party. Assuming you are in the political party that is pursuing your Worldview, then take a look at the candidate in the other party that you are consider voting for. If the reason you are voting for them is because you believe they will represent your Worldview, then that candidate is in the wrong party. In order for any individual to become accepted as a candidate in the wrong party, either they have to have been dishonest to the party members of the party they affiliated with, or they were manipulated into joining the other party – perhaps because they were a good vote getter. Either way, are you sure you want to place those naive or dishonest individuals in positions of power over society?

On the other hand, change for the sake of change is not change: Voting all the incumbents out when there are no established political criteria for selecting their replacements just guarantees the continuation of the same old same old, and – to make matters worse – you will be starting over with a group of totally inexperienced individuals.

Take a step back and take a good look at what is happening on the political scene. Do you know what your Worldview is? Are you sure you know where you are aiming? As a political foot soldier, your ammunition is your vote. Take aim! When you stand up to be counted, make sure you are standing with the right group and that that group has chosen the right candidate.

THINGS TO THINK ABOUT

"Direction"

The term "Direction" was used repetitively by Newt Gingrich and Republicans beginning in 1992. The Republican's "Direction" was opposed by President Clinton during his entire administration. You heard politicians on both sides talk about "Direction" in every campaign since. By now, one would think everyone in the United States would be able to explain the "Direction" each politician wants to take the country and describe the different "Directions" the country can go in. Can you? (Hint: There are only two Directions.)

"Change"

The country is echoing with the words, "We need a change."
The question is, "A change from What To What?"
Obama promised change.
Did we get it?
From what to what?
Some claim it was a change from a little of something
to a lot more of the same?
What are the alternatives?

One person's way of "Making Your Vote Count."

"I am only going to vote for someone that is going to win.
I am not going to waste my vote."[11]
Is the vote for someone that is not going to win a waste of a vote?

CHAPTER 4

REFLECT ON YOURSELF

You already have an opinion about how the world should work. It is your Worldview. But you also have political biases. The combination of your Worldview and your biases form your political beliefs. Your Worldview is founded on concepts which you may or may not be aware of or be able to cite. Your political biases are opinions that other people have manipulated you into accepting as the political gospel truth. The concepts upon which Worldviews are created is the subject of Chapter 5. In this chapter you will determine whether you were manipulated into embracing political biases.

Have You been Manipulated? Two tests are presented in this chapter: The Political Awareness Confusion (PAC) Factor test and the PAC Factor Confirmation Test. These two tests were designed to provide a crude measure of your current political astuteness. The PAC Factor test is intended to be a quick and honest assessment of what you truly believe concerning statements that have been made to you in the past. The responses you provide to yourself will create a baseline that will reflect your political astuteness. Answer the questions in the PAC Factor test with your honest initial 'gut' feelings. If you do, the PAC Factor test will provide useful insight into your current political biases. The PAC Factor Confirmation Test will confirm that your PAC Factor assessment of yourself has meaning. Take the PAC Factor Test again after you have finished the Political Primer and, if you have been true to yourself, you will find you have become politically wise – a Statesman.

PAC (Political Awareness Confusion) Factor Test
How easily are you politically manipulated? Find Out. Take this test.

Mark E. Glogowski, Ph.D.

Instructions: Place an X in the column to indicate whether you: A) strongly disagree, B) mildly disagree, C) mildly agree, D) strongly agree, or E) you neither agree nor disagree with each statement.

If you neither agree nor disagree – Stop! Be true to yourself.

Reflect on the statement until you choose A, B, C, or D.

Look! There is no "E" column!

Count the number of X's in each column. Multiply the number of x's in each column by the points indicated at the bottom of each column to determine the column total. Then add the column totals together. This is your PAC Factor.

PAC Factor Test

	A	B	C
	Strongly Disagree	Mildly Disagree	Mildly Agree
Step 1. Read the statement. Step 2. Then place an x in column A,B, C, or D on that row			
1. The deciding factor when voting should be how competent a candidate is, not the party to which a candidate belongs.			
2. Voting in the general election is more important than voting in a primary election.			
3. There is no difference between a Democrat and a Republican.			
4. All politicians are crooks.			
5. It doesn't matter who gets into office. All politicians are the same.			
6. You should always vote for the most qualified person for judge.			
7. Judges should not reveal their party affiliation, especially when running for office because party affiliation should be irrelevant.			
8. Democrats are Liberal and Republicans are Conservative.*			
9. The members of the Democrat and Republican parties should embrace the political views of their candidates.			

10. Political philosophy should not impact one's daily life.			
11. Political philosophy is important only during elections.			
12. It really doesn't matter if you register with a political party or to which party you belong.			
13. Political parties don't serve any real purpose.			
14. All candidates are the same.			
15. You should forget politics and stick to the issues.			
16. You should forget politics and stick to golf.			
Step 3. Count the number of x's in each column.			
POINTS	0	1	2
Step 4. Multiply the x count in each column as determined in Step 3 by the points indicated and place the total on this line for each column.			
Step 5. Add the column totals in Step 4 This is Your PAC factor			

The Political Primer

About Your PAC Factor. Your Political Awareness Confusion (**PAC**) factor is a variable reflecting your understanding of politics. The greater your political clarity and understanding of your Worldview, the lower will be your PAC Factor. As your PAC Factor goes down your political effectiveness will go up. What was your PAC factor? If you have not taken the PAC Factor Test, TAKE IT NOW!

Use the following PAC Factor scale to rank yourself.

PAC Factor Scale		
PAC Factor Score	PAC Factor Level	Political Rank★
0 to 1	1	Statesman
2 to 7	2	Politician
8 to 16	3	Partisan
17 to 24	4	Participant
25 to 29	5	Initiate
30 to 37	6	Victim
38 to 44	7	Stoolie
45 to 48	8	Stookie
<u>Definitions</u>★		
★These are the author's definitions as applied to the text of The Political Primer		
Statesman	A person preoccupied with the influence of Worldviews on society.	
Politician	A person that pursues consequences using their Worldview as a guide.	
Partisan	A person aware of Worldviews and the consequences of their pursuit.	
Participant	A person desiring to be involved, but does not fully accept political reality.	
Initiate	A person introduced to, but generally suspicious of politics.	
Victim	A person that naively and knowingly allows themself2 to be taken advantage of.	
Stoolie	A person who unknowingly is used and manipulated, often as a decoy.	
Stookie	A person easily bamboozled and unaware of what is happening.	

Mark E. Glogowski, Ph.D.

If you were honest with yourself when you took the PAC Factor test, your PAC factor score represents a quantitative measure of your inability to choose a candidate that will truly represent you after they get into office.

Know Yourself, Know Your Candidate. Even if you never gave any real serious thought about determining the political beliefs of other people, chances are pretty good that you have grappled with the question, "What do the Democratic, Republican, Conservative, Liberal, Libertarian, Reform, Independence, Green, and all the other political parties actually stand for?" If you rated a Victim, Stoolie, or Stookie on your PAC Factor test, your knee-jerk response might be to answer 'Not much'. Today, unfortunately, to a large extent you might be right. But, most politicians don't care. Politicians know that if they don't have the same Worldview as you, they will never represent you when they get into office. They also know that there is a high probability that they do not embrace your Worldview. But, they still want and need your vote, so their goal is to keep you from reflecting on your Worldview. That is why they enlist an army of Pawns to sway you. The Pawns, propagating PU statements, target everyone, playing on the emotional aspects of society's tragedies. The politician's campaign is therefore focused on brainwashing you. Using their Pawns, candidates try to manipulate you into supporting them any way they can. Pawns target everyone.

PU Power. What might surprise you is that, even if you can not elaborate on and clearly state your political beliefs, you are in fact very intransigent when it comes to your Worldview. No amount of facts in any argument will cause you to change your political beliefs on any issue without first addressing your Worldview. Your Worldview is your guide concerning what is right and what is not right. Elected officials are not different from you. They can not be guided by all four divergent Worldviews when they create a solution. Worldviews create uniquely different solutions. The elected official will consider three of those solutions to be wrong just as you will always consider three of the four Worldview solutions to be wrong. Which of the three Worldviews solutions are considered wrong depends upon which one of the Worldview solutions is considered right. When politicians choose, they choose one set of Worldview solutions. They have to, and they will, ignore all the other solutions. Candidates know that once in office they will pursue the solutions that create a structure for society that is consistent with their Worldview. Most likely you will never hear politicians state their intentions using "Worldview" terms, but since politicians can never truly represent the political beliefs of all the people whose support they are seeking, one fact is certain, politicians don't talk about their Worldviews – they won't talk about their Worldview during a campaign. If they did they would lose the votes of all those individuals that embrace one of the other three Worldviews!

What politicians and their campaign managers have figured out is that they can dupe people to gain their support. Politicians have found ways to get good people to set aside and ignore their personal Worldviews: To succeed, all they need to do is to deliberately propagate a smoke screen. PU statements are that smokescreen. PU statements conflict with a person's beliefs and belittle those people that have convictions. If you believe any PU statement, even briefly, the politician will succeed because you will not be able to recognize your Worldview through the political fog and smog of the PU statement. Ignoring your Worldview is the only condition under which you would support a candidate that advocates a solution that you would otherwise consider to be wrong. The PU statements are propagated specifically to get you to ignore your Worldview.

The reason the candidates do not talk about their solutions and do not give details of the solutions they intend to implement is that they do not want to take the chance that you will say to yourself "That should not be. That is not right." If a candidate manipulated you into abandoning your Worldview and you begin to reflect on what should be, you will begin to pursue your Worldview again. If that happens there is a high probability that you will stop supporting that political candidate that manipulated you. That is why the candidate's goal is to keep you emotional. They want to wear you out so that you will give up and leave it up to the candidate to create the solution. After all they are concerned about THE PROBLEM as much as you are. [Please recognize the sarcasm in that PU statement.]

Mark E. Glogowski, Ph.D.

Every successful utterance of a PU statement is followed with a play on the emotional aspects of society's tragedies, problems, and issues. The perpetrator of the PU statement will always make it clear that they have made some issue a priority and their opponent has not! You are then told what you are supposed to "feel" about their chosen, emotional, "most important" issue – THE PROBLEM. Candidates take advantage of the fact that if they are successful in manipulating you, the candidate that became associated with your negative feelings regarding THE PROBLEM is the candidate you do not vote for. When this happens, you have been manipulated.

To the extent that you strongly agree with any of the PU statements in the PAC Factor test, you are one of the targeted voters to be manipulated. The higher your PAC Factor test score, the greater the probability that you have been duped, and will be duped by candidates.

Confirmation of the PAC Factor Test. Doubt the validity of your PAC Factor ranking? The PAC Factor Confirmation Test will reaffirm your PAC Factor Test ranking. Look at your ranking on the PAC Factor test: Here is an assessment of how well you will fair in the PAC Factor Confirmation test. If you are a PAC Factor "Statesman" you live your political philosophy (Worldview) and you will find you believe you can answer all the questions in the PAC Factor Confirmation Test with ease. If you are a PAC Factor "Politician" you will have no difficulty believing you can provide an answer for most of the questions but perhaps not as convincingly as desired. If you are a PAC Factor "Partisan" you will feel comfortable answering completely at least one question and answering parts of the others. If you ranked a PAC Factor "Participant" you will feel comfortable answering only part of a couple of the questions in the PAC Factor Confirmation Test and will be unsure of the answers to the remaining questions. If you ranked a PAC Factor "Initiate" you will not feel comfortable answering any of the questions and may even become sarcastic when providing a response. If you ranked a PAC Factor "Victim" you will not be able to answer any of the questions. If you ranked a PAC Factor "Stoolie" you will probably have difficulty

The Political Primer

understanding the questions. As for you PAC Factor Stookies, No! We are not talking about sports.

Instructions for the PAC Factor Confirmation Test. Think about the questions in the PAC Factor Confirmation Test for a couple of minutes. You don't have to supply an actual answer. Just ask yourself, "If a good friend asked you the questions listed in the PAC Factor Confirmation Test and they wanted your honest input, do you believe you could provide a correct answer to the question?" Convincingly? Determine the confidence you have in your own ability to provide an accurate, rational answer for each question. Then place an X in the column that best reflects your confidence in your ability to provide your friend an answer.

Count the X's in each column. Multiply that count by the column points indicated and determine your column score. Add your column scores together. No points (0) are given if you have complete confidence in the answer you could provide. One point (1) is given for each answer you believe you could provide with a reasonable amount of confidence. Two points (2) for each answer you feel you would have some hesitation providing. Three points (3) if you have significant doubt you could answer the question to anyone's satisfaction. Four points (4) if you are completely unsure you could give an answer or if you don't completely and clearly understand the question.

PAC Factor Confirmation Test

	Very Confident	Reasonably Confident	Some Hesitation and doubt	Significant Doubt	Not a clue
1. Describe the difference in beliefs between a Democrat, Republican, Liberal, Conservative, and Moderate?					
2. What two questions should you ask a candidate in order to determine whether he or she will represent your political views?					
3. Can you identify the political (Democrat, Republican, Liberal, Conservative, and Moderate) bias in newspaper and broadcast news articles?					
4. Can you distinguish the effect a person's political philosophical beliefs have on their decisions from the influence the individual's personality traits have on their decisions?					
Column Totals					
Multiply Column Totals by these Points	0	1	2	3	4
Column Point Score					
Total Score (Add Column Point Scores)					

The Political Primer

Do the Math. If you multiply the PAC Factor Confirmation Test Score by 3 you should obtain a number approximately equivalent to your PAC Factor Test score. – generally plus or minus one classification. If the scores are dramatically different, review the list of Expectations for each classification. Where do you think you should have ranked? Were you honest with yourself when you answered the PAC Factor test?

About Your PAC Factor Confirmation Test Score. The lower your score, the better. The maximum score is 16.

Scoring your PAC Factor Confirmation Test	
If you Scored	Your Status
12 to 16	You probably feel absolutely lost when it comes to politics.
8 to 11	You have made a start toward understanding politics.
4 to 7	You most likely make a serious effort to understand politics.
0 to 3	Congratulations! Consider yourself politically astute.

Comments on Your PAC Factor and PAC Factor Confirmation Scores. If you are among the ranks of the Initiate, Victim, or Stoolie, you will most likely become disheartened as you become enlightened about politics. If you are one of these individuals, your first response to these tests will probably be to begin to discount the ideas discussed in this Primer. Make no mistake about it, you have been duped, and you are not alone. You have been duped by people who have passed off one line PU statements as political wisdom. The statements that make up the foundation of the PAC Factor test have been propagated over the years by your parents, friends, and even prominent and well-meaning candidates and campaign managers. Your parents and friends are probably suffering from the same malady you struggle with; they are politically immature and are themselves political Initiates, Victims, or Stoolies. If anyone gives you a one line PU statement as the answer for anything, it is probably because they don't understand the basics of politics – or perhaps they do and they are attempting to manipulate you.

They need your Vote. Candidates and campaign managers need your vote. On the chance you do not embrace their Worldview, well-meaning candidates will deliberately attempt to manipulate you into voting for them because they really believe they will represent you, or naively believe they are your best choice regardless of your Worldview. After all, haven't they convinced you that they are concerned about the same PROBLEM you are concerned about? *[NOTE TO THE READER: The last question is again intentionally sarcastic. The only condition under which you would ever believe a candidate who does not share your Worldview will represent you is when you are a victim of the candidate's successful use of a PU statement!]*

Well Meaning or Not, Here They Come. The one line PU statements are deliberately propagated by well-meaning and not so well-meaning candidates. Both deliberately try to sway people who have embraced Worldviews the candidate believes to be wrong. The candidate intends to ignore these people once in office. So, well meaning or not so well meaning, the purpose of the one-line PU statements is always the same: To get you to abandon your Worldview and vote for a candidate that is pursuing a different Worldview.

The effectiveness of the one-line PU statements resides in the fact that, if you even subconsciously accept the PU statements as being valid, you have told yourself that your Worldview is irrelevant.

PU Statements: Political Untruths and Politically Unrelated Statements. Take another look at the statements in the PAC Factor Test. Haven't you heard all these statements before? The one-line **P**olitical **U**ntruths are intended to trash your thought process with unfounded emotions. They are intended to belittle your personal convictions. If you believe a PU statement, even for a brief moment, you will experience meaningless feelings of disgust. The power of these statements resides in the fact that the statements are readily accepted as gospel by the political Victim, Stoolie, and Stookie. Many political Initiates, and Participants also easily succumb to the power of the PU statement, causing these individuals to abandon any glimmer of understanding of their Worldviews that they may have been developing. If you are subjected to PU statements often enough you will be overwhelmed with negative emotions whenever people discuss politics.

> "All politicians are the same"
> "All politicians are crooks"
> "Vote for the individual, not the party"
> "Never talk politics or religion"

There are hundreds of Political Untruths that have been propagated.

The Politically Unrelated statements are another form of PU statement made for the same reason: To get you to abandon your Worldview. They include such statements as:

> "The candidate is well qualified."
> "The candidate is a long time supporter that deserves a chance."
> "The candidate is well connected."
> "The candidate is well funded."

Politically Unrelated statements are justifications that, while they may be true, they cover any conceivable subject matter or concept except those concepts related to the foundation of the Worldviews. This second type of PU statement is the favorite of political party leaders when their selected candidate does not embrace the party's Worldview. Beware of both types of PU statements.

Abandoning your Biases. PU statements are just a tool deliberately used to manipulate people. Once you are convinced of this fact you will stop allowing the PU statements to trash your Worldview beliefs and you will begin to abandon your biases. Recognizing PU statements for what they are is an essential first

step in beginning to understand your Worldview and how your Worldview relates to the political parties. When PU statements no longer have an impact on you, you will stop suppressing your Worldview, you will begin to understand the Worldviews of each political party, and you will recognize the structure that each party is striving to construct for society. You will become confident in your ability to choose candidates that will represent you – just by their choice of words. Once PU statements no longer have an influence on you, you will begin to realize that your Worldview plays a major role in your personal daily life, even with your family and friends.
Take Your PAC Factor to Zero. When you finish reading this Political Primer, take the PAC Factor test again. Your PAC Factor should be dramatically reduced, perhaps even to zero.

The goal of most political campaigns today is to get you to abandon your Worldview and to vote for a candidate who does not share your Worldview.

CHAPTER 5

THE POLITICAL INTERROGATORIES.

The Right Worldview, The Right Solution. Your Worldview is the single most important piece of political information you can discover. It determines how you believe society should work. Any solution that is consistent with your Worldview you will consider to be a right solution.

How Worldviews are Determined. Worldviews are determined by answering the Political Interrogatories presented below. These interrogatories are questions that have no right or wrong answer. There are just answers. Your answers! The four combinations of answers to the two Political Interrogatories each represent a different Worldview. Your answers are the foundation of your Worldview – your political philosophy. Three other Worldviews exist. Those, you will find, you consider to be wrong Worldviews for society to follow. You will consider to be wrong every solution that supports any Worldview other than yours. However, anyone who answers the Political Interrogatories differently believes in one of the other three Worldviews. They will consider your Worldview to be one of the three wrong Worldviews and they will consider any solution derived from your Worldview to be wrong.

You might now begin to see a problem developing: If Worldviews are generated from the Political Interrogatories and no answer to a Political Interrogatory is a right or wrong answer, and if each combination of answers generates a different Worldview, then aren't all Worldviews equally valid. How do you determine which Worldview is the right Worldview?

The answer to that question is: The Worldview that is the right Worldview is your Worldview. It is your choice. That is why politics is all about <u>you</u>!

Don't tell me what I Believe! You are probably now saying to yourself, this author has not said anything yet and I'm not going to let him, or anyone else for that matter, tell me what I believe. Be reassured, you have already determined your Worldview. All that is about to happen is that you are going to learn about Worldviews and you will determine which Worldview you have already chosen to embrace. Provided, that is, if when the Political Interrogatories are presented, you answer them for yourself. If you do you will soon realize those answers are the standard you use daily. Those answers are the foundation upon which you determine what you believe is right and what you believe is wrong in the world. They determine how you believe people should act and interact, and how governments should act and interact with their citizens and with other governments.

Where do you Start? It is absolutely futile to start with questions phrased: *"What is my political philosophy?"* or, *"What do I believe?"*, or *"What is my Worldview?"* If you start with these questions you end up giving yourself a contrived answer that is based on what you heard other people say – most of which is just a bunch of hooey influenced by PU statements.

Start with the basics. Your experiences, consciously and subconsciously, caused you to develop beliefs about Reality – how the world works. As you learned what could be, and then evaluated what you experienced, you developed your Worldview. Your political beliefs are based on these two decisions: What you decided is your Reality and what you decided is your Worldview. What you want to happen politically is dependant upon whether your Reality is in agreement with your Worldview.

The Starting Point. This Political Primer is based on the premise that two universal concepts, Expectation and Responsibility, are contemplated by every adult without exception. Just as those two concepts formed your Reality, setting Expectations for how people should interact and determining who should be given the authority to make decisions is the starting point for the development of your Worldviews.

Expectations and Responsibility: A Brief Review. Reflect for a bit on any interaction you had with another individual. It won't matter whether the incident you reflect on involved a parent, spouse, child, neighbor, or stranger. It also won't matter whether the incident was planned or spontaneous. Consider the moments just before the start of the interaction. Did you not immediately, even if just for a brief moment, struggle consciously or unconsciously with the following type of questions: Do you know the individual – or not? Do you expect a good outcome from the pending interaction – or a bad outcome? Should you take a defensive position right from the start – or wait? Will you exhibit Good Will and give the benefit of the doubt if a wrong statement or misdoing is perceived? Then what? The list of potential questions concerning your safety is almost endless. Never-the-less, for every pending interaction with other people, you always establish an Expectation for the outcome before the interaction starts.

No. You usually do not actually ask yourself questions. What you usually do is just provide answers to yourself in the form of thoughts that went something like, "Hey! It is _____. I haven't seen them for years. This is great!" or "Oh crap! It is _____ again. I better bite my tongue. Maybe I can avoid them." Consciously or unconsciously, you established Expectations concerning the pending interactions and those Expectations then guided you in your conduct. The more hazardous the pending interaction was perceived to be, the more conscious the decision concerning the Expectation that you set.

During the brief interlude prior to a pending interaction you also determine who would make decisions during the interaction: The reality is, either you or they make the decision(s) if any are made.

After the interaction, you said to yourself, either consciously or unconsciously, "That was a good interaction. I'm glad we met." Or, "Gad! I hope we don't meet again soon!" or something in between. Upon evaluation of the incident, if a decision was made, you said consciously or unconsciously, "They made a good decision." Or, "That was not a good decision." Or, "I hope they like the decision I made." Or "I should not have made that decision." Based on the decisions that were made you would have arrived at a conclusion concerning the people or person you met with: They are basically Good people or they are basically Evil people. That's your Reality

Having evaluated Reality, if everything went as you predicted, Reality was as it should be. However, to the extent that the wrong person made the decision or that the responses in the interactions were not as you projected them to be, Reality did not agree with your Worldview of how the interaction should have gone. So what should have happened? What Direction should the interaction have gone? Who should have been Responsible to be the ultimate decision maker? Were the decisions made appropriate for the Evil nature of the people involved? Were they appropriate for the Good Will and Good intentions of the people involved?

During your formative years when you interacted with other people you did not need to be concerned about Direction. Direction was not an issue or a problem. Nearly everyone else had authority over you. It was your parents, your teacher, your minister, your guardian ... , the list seemed endless because, as a child, society did not give you any authority to make decisions. You were not Responsible.

But, eventually you found that others wanted you to make decisions and become Responsible. You began to decide quickly, going into every interaction, whether you would transfer Responsibility and authority to another person or group, or retain Responsibility and authority for yourself[13]. Most of each person's teen years are spent determining how to resolve the Responsibility issue.

Your assessments of pending interactions eventually became just your way of viewing the world – your Reality. Today, your Expectation for any pending interaction is always dependant upon your perception of the Good or Evil intentions of other individual(s) and who you believe is going to be the Responsible authority.

Consciously or unconsciously, prior to every encounter, you still struggle with the two concepts, "Responsibility" and "Expectation". These fundamental concepts, the subject of Dr Harris' book, I'm OK. You're OK, permeate every aspect of your life. Your assessment of a situation, as well as the assessment by others, happens so automatically and so fast that the process is often just a gut feeling, a personal prejudice, an instinct. That assessment is essential because in extreme situations your spontaneous assessments can mean the difference between survival and the other less desirable option.

But what happens when the Reality of what happens does not match your Expectation: What if what happens "just should not be"? You immediately reflect on what happened. What Direction did the conversation go in? Who made the decision? Who should have been Responsible to make the decision?

Direction and Approach. Direction is about who should have the Responsibility and authority to make decisions. Approach concerns your Expectations of Good or Evil occurring. The first Political Interrogatory deals with the concept of Responsibility. Your answer to the First Political Interrogatory determines the "Direction" you want society to go in. As a consequence of choosing a Direction you will find that you embrace either the Democrat's or the Republican's "Direction". The second Political Interrogatory deals with the concept of Approach. Your answer to the second Political Interrogatory will determine the Approach that you believe society should take based on your Expectation and whether your Expectations focus on the Good or on the Evil that will occur. As a consequence of choosing an Approach you will find you embrace either a Conservative or a Liberal "Approach".

The answers to the Political Interrogatories create unique combinations of Direction and Approach, and those combinations result in the four distinct Worldviews. Direction and Approach are important because, as will be discussed in detail latter, Direction and Approach, together, are the structure of society: In order to create a solution for any problem, both 'Direction' and 'Approach' must be selected prior to creating the solution.

Your combination of answers to the Political Interrogatories identifies the Direction and Approach you desire society to pursue. To you, your selected Direction and Approach is the right Direction and the right Approach for the creation of a right solution to every problem. Any other combination of Direction and Approach will result in the creation of a wrong solution.

Mark E. Glogowski, Ph.D.

If you Disagree. If you find the two Interrogatories below place you in a political category that is contrary to where you currently think you belong, you probably have been duped. If your answers to the two Political Interrogatories associate you with a Worldview other than the Worldview of the party you are currently affiliated with, keep reading. The choice of which of the four Worldviews that you actually embraced is more important than the Worldview of the party you affiliated with. Worldviews are used to create society's structure. The political parties pursue the placement of individuals in positions of power and control over society who will use their Worldview to create solutions. The Worldviews of those individuals will create a structure for society that will cause the features of society to rearrange. Their solutions will determine how individuals and government thereafter interact. That is why the choice of which of the four Worldviews that you actually embraced is important. You get to pick the people that are placed in those positions of control over of society. What is your Worldview? If it is not the same as the Worldview being pursued by the party you are in, are you supporting the right party with the right candidates?

The First Political Interrogatory

Who is ultimately responsible for the welfare of the individual?

Cataclysmic Events. An assumption had been made in the past by the author that one of the roles of government was to take charge during disasters, such as the cataclysmic occurrences of war, famine, floods, and earthquakes. Believing this to be the case, the introduction of the first Political Interrogatory was always preceded by a conditional statement, such as, "When you answer this question do not consider disasters which will leave the individual helpless." To the author's surprise, after hurricane Katrina, in 2007, politicians and government officials stated that during a national disaster, and for at least three days thereafter, there is little the government can do to help the individual; officials even issued decrees stating people have the responsibility to prepare, plan, and fend for themself prior to, during, and immediately after such calamities. Some people agree and some people disagree with this decree, so obviously, the first Political Interrogatory is applicable even under cataclysmic events. For the moment, however, lets side step the issue of responsibility during cataclysmic events and consider the first Political Interrogatory from the perspective of an average person living a normal uneventful life with all of the opportunity and riches that the world can and does provide. Barring any major calamity, "Who is ultimately responsible for the welfare of the individual?"

Food, Clothing, and Shelter. Should the average healthy American be responsible for the food, clothing, and shelter for themselves and their family? Should they plan and save for their own retirement? Or, should  the government be responsible to provide for the welfare of the average American? Is it the individual's Responsibility to seek and to provide for their own health care, or should the government provide health care for everyone? If an individual is unfortunate enough to need aid and assistance for food, clothing, and shelter, should the aid come primarily and directly from the efforts of other individuals, charities, and religious groups, or should the government be the major provider of aid to individuals? Should parents be responsible for providing for the health and welfare of their children and determine when and what health care they receive, or should the government make those decisions? What about you? Do you want to independently provide for yourself and your family, or do you want the government to provide for you? Using labels already prevalent in politics:

If you believe the government should be ultimately responsible for the welfare of the individual, you are a Democrat.

If you believe the individual should be ultimately responsible for their own welfare, you are a Republican.

Democratic and Republican Party Members' Shared beliefs. If you ask members of the Democratic and Republican parties the first Political Interrogatory, the majority of the individuals in each party will provide you with the answer indicated. The first Political Interrogatory truly segments the common belief of the majority of individuals in each of these two parties. If this interrogatory is answered honestly, this interrogatory will also identify some of the individuals in each political party that are considered "Moderates".

NOTE TO READER: Moderates are individuals that have joined a political party but do not share the Worldview of the other party members. They are pursuing a different Worldview. Moderates are discussed briefly in Chapter 7 and are the subject of Chapter 26.

The Second Political Interrogatory

Are people inherently Good or inherently Evil?

A Sliding Scale. The second Political Interrogatory is a sliding scale question. The initial answer you provide may depend more upon what kind of day you are having than your Worldview. So, before you answer, consider the following few examples: If you lost your wallet and someone found it, would you expect that it would be returned to you with the contents of the wallet intact? Obviously, you have to be a realist and acknowledge that there are dishonest people in society that will just take the money. There are also some people who are down and out and despite their best initial intentions they will spend the money on their own survival. As a realist you would also recognize that there are down and out people who would never consider taking the money and would return the wallet intact. The question is, what do you believe is the probability that you will never see your wallet or your money? If you acknowledge the existence of both dishonest people and down and out people, what is your Expectation of the actions of the rest, the majority of the people? Do you believe there is a 100% chance that your wallet and money will not be returned? Would the majority of the people in America return the wallet? Perhaps your Expectation is that the average person finding your wallet would take your money and return the wallet with the credit cards, expecting to receive a reward. It depends on chance as to who found your wallet. So, ask yourself, what if the person that found your wallet represented the average American? Would you expect, as well as hope, that the average American would return the wallet. Or, would you expect and relegate yourself to the fact that the average American would pilfer your wallet and toss the remains in the garbage?

OK. Now try the question from this perspective: Do you consider yourself to be an average American? Do other people consider you to be an average American? What would you do?

Your answer to this question establishes primarily what you believe is Reality, not what you truly believe about how the world should work.

How Difficult the Task Is. What the example of the lost wallet reveals is that it is often difficult to separate your Worldview from Reality, especially when an issue hits close to home. Didn't you say to yourself something like, 'I know the way the world should work: Whoever finds my wallet should return it to me. But, that is just not real life!'

Politics deals with 'how the world should work', so let's dig a little deeper and consider other issues.

Crime Issues. How should society deal with crime? Should government view people as basically Good and work to improve education, provide opportunities for troubled individuals to obtain counseling, create incentives for people to work, get more people involved in their community? Or, do you believe the solution to the crime problem is to hire more police, create new laws, and enforce laws more strictly because that is the only way to deal with basically Evil people?

Its Your Choice. How about other issues? Should people have total freedom of choice over what they do, say, buy, read and see? Or, should restrictions be placed on people's actions because of the violence in society? Should there be less regulation of businesses or more regulation of businesses? Should we relax our laws so that government doesn't make criminals out of the average citizen, or create new laws limiting people's options because of the general degradation of society's moral standard? Would you be in favor of, or opposed to, tougher laws and stricter law enforcement to stabilize and improve society? What is your choice?

The Approach. If your Expectation is that your lost wallet should be returned intact, that improving people's lives is the proper way to reduce crime, that an emphasis  should be placed on freedom of choice, or that stricter law enforcement is not the approach we should take to reduce crime, it is because you believe people are inherently Good. If your Expectation is that you would never see your lost wallet again, that more police and stricter laws are required to reduce crime, or that there should be restrictions on people's choices, it is because you believe people are inherently Evil. The Approach you prefer for any solution is dependant upon whether you are looking at the Good that people can do or anticipating the Evil that they can perpetrate.

One last question. The above examples are on a sliding scale, and for the most part your answer is dependant upon whether you are having a good day or a bad day, or whether the issue hits close to home. This next question is not on a sliding scale. What is more important: The letter of the law or the intent of the law?

If you believe the letter of the law is more important, you approach the law from the point of view that people are basically Evil and since they make bad decisions they should not be allowed to make their own independent decisions regarding what is intended by the law.

If you believe the intent of the law is more important, you acknowledge that laws can not be written that anticipate all of the unique, individualized circumstances around every type of incident. People should be allowed a degree of individual judgment, depending on their individual circumstances, and as long as they are following the intent of the law, because people are basically Good.

Using currently applicable political terminology:

If you believe people are basically inherently Good, you are a Liberal.

If you believe people are basically inherently Evil, you are a Conservative.

Shared Beliefs of Liberal and Conservative Party Members. The majority of individuals in the Liberal and Conservative parties will agree with the assigned beliefs as indicated. The application of the terms Liberal and Conservative to the answers to the second Political Interrogatory is consistent with the historical political use of the words Liberal and Conservative. For the remainder of this text, the definitions of Liberal and Conservative will be employed as determined by the Political Interrogatories. The two terms will relate to whether you are approaching a problem and the solution to the problem from the point of view that people are basically Evil and they cannot be given free reign in their choices (Conservative) or from the point of view that people are basically Good and should be allowed to choose and pursue their own solutions (Liberal).

The Political Interrogatories argue against the statements made by political commentators that imply all Democrats are Liberals and all Republicans are Conservatives.

Conservative Values. Some ideas currently being touted as "Conservative Values" have nothing to do with being politically Conservative. Also, some "Liberal Values" have nothing to do with being politically Liberal. Confusion is being propagated, often deliberately, by talk show hosts in order to create the "Us versus Them" atmosphere that the talk show hosts revel in.

Don't Fret. Did you find yourself conflicted in the above examples? Do you believe that some problems are more appropriate to approach from the perspective that people are inherently Good but that some problems are more appropriate to approach from the perspective that people are inherently Evil? Did you find yourself saying, "I know I would like to believe people are basically Good because you can meet the nicest people. But reality is a rude awakener. Whether it is timing or unfortunate coincidences, there are days when it would be hard to believe there are any Good people left in the world." Well, don't abandon your Worldview beliefs because of reality. Your Reality and your reality are not always in agreement with each other, and your Reality is not always in agreement with your Worldview. Your Worldview, Reality and reality are separate concepts. When answering the second Political Interrogatory it is important to acknowledge that the perception of Good and Evil is on a moving scale in reality, and reality is an environment beyond our control. Nevertheless, established in your mind is a belief of whether the majority of people are Good or are Evil. That viewpoint, your Reality, is fixed and it is not easily changed. That is why phrases like 'a large dose of reality', or 'taken with a grain of salt' (or a pound of salt, or a ton of salt) exist and are used. They help us to accommodate exceptions so that we don't have to change our Worldview or our concept of Reality.

The Political versus the Fiscal. Most people already grasp the difference between political definitions of Liberal and Conservative versus the fiscal use of the terms "liberal" and "conservative". But, to drive the point home, consider the following example: If a multi-billion dollar proposal is placed before congress to create new jails, a Conservative politician, one that believes people are inherently Evil, would be in favor of such a program and become liberal in their support of how much revenue should be allocated for the program. A Liberal politician would oppose such a program as a waste of government resources and would become conservative concerning how much money should be allocated.

Alternatively, a program to initiate new social events or social programs, such as increased welfare allocations to the poor, the Conservative would become very conservative in their willingness to support what they would consider to be a wasteful program, while the Liberal (specifically the Liberal Democrat, because Liberal Republicans would not embrace a government program) would advocate a liberal allocation to 'such a worthy project'. As is customary in writing, as just illustrated, the use of the terms conservative and liberal when dealing with issues related to money and time will be printed with lower case letters.

The Liberal versus Conservative Approach. Whether you take a Liberal versus Conservative Approach is a decision concerning whether a solution is to be created from the perspective of addressing and empowering Good individuals (Liberal) or from the perspective of containing Evil individuals (Conservative). If you approach the development of laws and regulations from the viewpoint that everyone is basically Evil, then you create the rules, guidelines, regulations, and laws around which everyone is to live their lives. Even if no one was injured, damaged, or offended, a Conservative would support severely punishing those that step outside the written letter of the law simply because the individual violated the law. If you approach the development of laws and regulations from the viewpoint that everyone is basically Good, you preserve personal choice and resist the temptation to create laws that place unnecessary limitations on everyone just to protect them from the careless and inconsiderate few. The Liberal's goal is to preserve choice for basically Good people. While the Liberal would not support punishing an individual just because the individual violated the law, the Liberal will support punishment of careless and inconsiderate individuals if they deliberately and intentionally break society's trust and in doing so harm you or another.

The Irony and a Conundrum. Here is the irony and a conundrum of the Liberal and Conservative viewpoints. To the Conservative, justice cannot be had unless people follow the letter of the law. If people are not following the letter of the law, even when doing so is contrary to the intent of the law, they are law breakers, and thus Evil. To the Liberal, the intent of the law is of utmost importance and to ignore the intent of the law, the very reason the law was created, leads to injustice. While Conservatives believe everyone is inherently Evil, they follow the letter of the law, and by following the letter of the law Conservatives support the Liberals position that everyone is inherently Good, even Conservatives. Liberals, on the other hand, feel justified at times violating the letter of the law as long as they stay within the intent of the law. In doing so they thereby support the Conservative's view that everyone is inherently Evil, including the so called Good intentioned Liberals.

Mark E. Glogowski, Ph.D.

Do you Drive? Here is one last test to determine if you truly are a Liberal or Conservative. Do you drive? If so, do you follow the letter of the law and never drive over the speed limit no matter what, or do you follow the intent of the law and exceed the speed limit when you feel the road conditions, traffic conditions, the excellent condition of your car, and your desire to arrive at your destination a little bit earlier all justify a higher speed?

Two Political Interrogatories.
The pillars around which political philosophy is constructed.

The First Political Interrogatory

Who is ultimately responsible for the welfare of the individual?

The Second Political Interrogatory

Are people inherently good or inherently evil?

CHAPTER 6

FOUR POLITICAL PHILOSOPHIES

Are you uncomfortable with the result from your answers to the Political Interrogatories that cause you to be classified as a Democrat and Liberal, or a Democrat and Conservative, or a Republican and Liberal, or a Republican and Conservative? If your current party affiliation was the result of an arbitrary decision, you may be one of the many individuals that are registered with the Republican party but are identified by the first Political Interrogatory as being a Democrat, or one of the many individuals registered with the Democratic party that are identified by the first Political Interrogatory as being a Republican. This is most likely the situation if your party affiliation was the result of a decision of convenience; you merely joined the party that ____ belonged to. (Fill in the blank with your parent's name, a friend's name, a town's name, etc . . .) To the politically astute, if you are registered with the wrong party, you stand out at party functions like a cat in a canary cage!

Political Fundamentals. The two concepts expressed by the Political Interrogatories are basic fundamental political philosophy determining concepts. When other people disagree with you on an issue, you can determine their Worldview by reflecting on the Direction and Approach of their proposed solution. Once you are able to determine the influence that their Worldview had on their solution, you will begin to understand why, when the disagreement is based on a fundamental difference in Worldviews, that there can not be and should not be a bipartisan compromise on the solution. Politics is not a game. Your Worldview is not something you should ever compromise. When you compromise your Worldview you are assisting in the creation of a structure for society that will cause society to become a society that you do not want to live in!

Ambiguity is Deliberate. People refer to "Liberal Democrat" and "Conservative Republican" primarily because there is a political need for both a Direction and an Approach. The names of four current political parties, Liberal, Conservative, Republican, and Democrat, do not reflect a complete political philosophy covering both Direction and Approach. The Liberal and Conservative parties are organized around an Approach. What is their Direction? To whom do they intend to give the authority to make decisions? The Democratic and Republican parties are organized around a Direction. What is their Approach to any problem? These are the labels of today's major political parties. Party leaders will claim this ambiguity is good because it allows them to solicit support from other parties and it allows them to find common ground with people in the other parties as they seek support for candidates or try to pass bills. The current party labels today are not intended to help you, the voter. They are intended to help the party leaders play politics fast and furious, the way politicians like to pay politics. Since the party labels do not identify a complete political philosophy with both Direction and Approach, politicians feel justified in using PU statements to achieve their goals; because everyone, even you, can be exasperated to confusion and then be easily manipulated.

Today's Two Party (Two Worldview) System. Two of the Political Interrogatory determined political groups, the Liberal Democrat and Conservative Republican, have become the dominant groups in the Democratic and Republican parties, respectively. The dominance in these parties of Liberal Democrat and Conservative Republican members, respectively, is the justification the talk show hosts and news media commentators use to rationalize the use of the term "Liberal" as a synonym to refer to Democratic party members and "Conservative" as a synonym for Republican party members.

The Democrats today are aggressively moving in the Direction of having government provide a solution to every problem in society. They have taken a Liberal Approach to achieve their political goals. They have no difficulty demanding the resources from the public for the government to use. They freely exercise government's powers to implement their solutions. And, they provide as many choices and options as is possible.

Republicans today oppose that Direction and stress the importance of the individual taking care of themself and making their own decisions. But the Republicans are pursuing their Direction from a Conservative Approach, which concerns itself with the protection of the public from harmful acts of the individual, as well as protecting the individual from themself. The Republican's Conservative Approach is to insure that individuals do not make unacceptable decisions and choices. To accomplish that goal Conservative Republicans provide as much government guidance as they deem is needed. They do so in the form of rules, regulations, and codes, and they create the required agencies with the authority to enforce compliance.

The Democratic and Republican parties have fully embraced the Worldview of the Liberal Democrat and the Conservative Republican. In the current two party system in the United States the Liberal Republican and the Conservative Democrat are without a political home.

A Four Party System. Many individuals classified as Conservative Democrat and Liberal Republican have already left the Democratic and Republican parties. They left not because of the Direction the parties were headed. They left because of the Approach adopted by the two dominant parties was inconsistent with the beliefs of the Conservative Democrats and the Liberal Republicans. Two relatively new parties have sprung up: The Reform Party and the Libertarian Party.

The Reform party's by-laws and constitution are consistent with the Direction that government is responsible for the welfare of its citizens and its Approach is that government should implement solutions to society's problems whether the people want them or not because people are basically Evil. The Reform party openly pursues the restriction of individual freedoms in their proposed solutions. The Reform party's Approach to government appeals to Conservative Democrats who believe the current Approach to solving society's problems being taken by the Liberal Democrats is too wish-washy.

Mark E. Glogowski, Ph.D.

The Libertarian party's by-laws and constitution is consistent with the concept that people are basically Good and that government should support the rights of the individual to make their own decisions. They advocate little or no government interference or involvement in the affairs of the individual's daily life. Libertarians believe each citizen is responsible for their own welfare and the welfare of the individuals in their charge. Their goal is to create a government that will responsibly insure that individual liberties are protected and that the individual's resources are not confiscated by others or by the government itself. To the Libertarian, the Republican party today is adversely and wrongfully restricting the rights and opportunities of individuals and impairing the ability of individuals to take care of themselves and their families.

Four Worldviews; Four Political Parties. The stage is set. There exists four political parties in the United States with each party embracing a Worldview rejected by the other three parties. These Worldviews, easily identified by the two Political Interrogatories, create distinct and unique political objectives for the creation of a structure for society. Today, in the United States', the four Political Interrogatory determined Worldviews are separately embraced by the Democratic, Republican, Libertarian, and Reform parties. This is the new political reality in the United States: Four basic political philosophies, each pursuing a different structure for our society. The relationships of the four political parties to the Political Interrogatory Worldviews are depicted in the Table 6-1

Table 6-1
Four Basic Categories of Political Beliefs

Are People Inherently Good or Inherently Evil?	Who is Ultimately Responsible for the Welfare of the Individual?	
	Government	Individual
Inherently Good	*Liberal Democrat* **Democratic Party**	*Liberal Republican* **Libertarian Party**
Inherently Evil	*Conservative Democrat* **Reform Party**	*Conservative Republican* **Republican Party**

A Warning. Having identified your Worldview, the question you will need to ask yourself is whether you should continue to support the political party that you are affiliated with. If you find yourself affiliated with a political party that does not share your Worldview, you will find that the majority of the party members believe your solutions to be wrong. They are pursuing the establishment of a structure for society contrary to your Worldview. Your continued membership in such a party will be counterproductive to your own inner desires, and your membership will result in you supporting the construction of a structure for a society that you do not want to live in! If, while you are a member of this party you become a candidate for any office, support from party members will not be there on Election Day because the party members embrace a Worldview different from your Worldview. But then, you probably already suspected this to be true based on the number of heated discussions you have experienced.

On the other hand, your association with a party that embraces your Worldview will be productive and as a candidate you can expect to receive the full support of the party's members.

Third Parties. Numerous parties have sprung up for a variety of reasons. Most of these parties fail to provide a Direction or an Approach. Often both Direction and Approach are missing. When the third parties are not clearly philosophically affiliated with one of the other major parties, or they simply become issue oriented, the third party will default to the Direction and Approach of the Conservative Democrat Worldview: Third parties give government the Responsibility to impose solutions whether the Evil people want them or not. The imposed caveat, however, is always:

"... as long as the government is following the criteria _____ demanded by the third party."

Fill in the blank. The criteria usually relates to 'THE PROBLEM". When a third party is affiliated with a major party, generally indicated by the cross endorsement of some or all of the candidates, the Direction and Approach of the third party is that of the major party.

Emphasizing the Difference. The dramatic difference between Liberal and Conservative approaches to government is best illustrated by comparing the solutions created for the examples in Part 2. Upon reviewing those examples you will realize that Liberal Democrats and Conservative Republicans share much in common and that Conservative Democrat and Liberal Republican share nothing in common.

ENFORCER

　　　DEFENDER

　　　　　CONTROLLER

　　　　　　　ADVOCATE

CHAPTER 7

FOUR NEW POLITICAL TERMS

The Purpose of Political Parties. Political parties bring together people of like mind. They create a pool of voting power with the objective of getting candidates elected who will pursue the same Worldview held by the party's members. The goal is to select candidates that will create a structure for society that is consistent with the party's Worldview. A lot of people haven't figured this out. They believe people should not belong to, and should not support, political parties.

The two major political parties, the Democratic Party and the Republican Party, are each currently focusing on just one Direction and one Approach. The consequence has been that the political parties have lost membership. Even when the individuals that left these parties could not explain the details of their personal Worldview, those individuals somehow knew their personal Worldview was no longer consistent with the Worldview the party was pursuing.

The parties have also lost membership for another reason: The parties have been nominating candidates that do not embraced the Worldview Direction and Approach of the party. And again, even though the individuals that left these parties could not explain their personal political Worldview beliefs, they too somehow knew that the party's chosen candidates would not work to create a society that the individual wanted to live in. When a political party continuously chooses candidates that do not embrace the party's Worldview the result is confusion. No one knows why the party even exists – there is no clear purpose, or goal. No wonder people claim they believe you should not belong to a political party and claim you should vote for the individual and not the party.

Mark E. Glogowski, Ph.D.

Unfortunately, those individuals not affiliated with a political party will not be politically effective. When they realize they are not politically effective, some people will pursue current political wisdom suggested activities in an effort to increase their political influence and just agitate. Some people will arbitrarily join one of the four major political parties; these individuals have a one out of four chance of joining the right party. Some people will join newly created third parties in the hopes of influencing the new party from the ground up. But, with no clear understanding of their own Worldview, what possible help can they give a third party that has embraced no Worldview? Some ambitious people will form a new political party. Again, without a clear understanding of what their personal Worldview is, what possible chance do they have of creating a solid foundation for their new party? Never-the-less, a number of these individuals, with a desire to be heard, have actually formed such foundationless parties: The Tea Parties and "No-Label" parties are examples. The Tea Party with their "Throw the incumbents out" rhetoric and the No-Label party with their 'Down with Labels' rhetoric chant their PU statements as mantras in the hopes of persuading other people to abandon their Worldviews. THEY want you to 'Come. Follow THEM!' The problem is, no one knows what THEY stand for. What kind of society THEY are trying to create or preserve? Just look at the political commentator's assessment of what the Tea Party stands for. ...aaahhh ... don't know! What does the No-Label party stand for ... aaahhh ... anything, as long as you don't put a label on it!

In time, if these independent voters discover their Worldview they will join the party that embraces their personal Worldview. In the meantime, what all of these politically lonesome individuals share in common is what they are not: They are not Liberal; they are not Conservative; they are not Democrat; and they are not Republican. They are something else. Until a lightening bolt of genius hits, they will remain a 'No-Label', 'independent', 'tea partying', 'concerned citizen', voter who believes that they are keeping all of their options open. These people are fairly easy to spot as they pass by because they shout their mantras, a litany of PU statements, like a fog horn warning of a potential danger.

They call out to the world, through the fog and smog of a 'politics as usual' mentality, hoping someone will hear them, hoping that they will do some good: They stand on some lonely shoreline of politics, calling out, aware of the danger but not knowing what to do. They will be picked off, one by one, by the political Pawns and the political professionals. If and when any of these individuals associated with the No-Label party or the Tea Party, or any third party, finally take the time to answer the Political Interrogatories for themself they will quickly learn what it is that they politically believe. When that happens the political skies will clear for them and the right course of action will become obvious.

It is a Matter of Time. It is both unfortunate and fortunate that talk show hosts make an effort to identify all Democrats as Liberal Democrats, and all Republicans as Conservative Republicans. It is unfortunate because the implication is that any Republican that is not a Conservative and any Democrat that is not a Liberal is mentally unstable. What is fortunate about the ridged labeling by the media is that the Democratic party is now comprised mostly of Liberal Democrats pursuing the "Liberal Democrat" Worldview, thus making the statement fairly accurate that all 'Democrats' are Liberal. Most, if not all, Conservative Democrats have left the Democratic party. The same phenomenon is happening in the Republican party. With the percentage of Conservative Republicans in the Republican party increasing, because the Republican party is aggressively pursuing a Conservative Republican Worldview, most 'Republicans' are now Conservative. In time, individuals that left the Democratic and Republican parties will find the Reform party or the Libertarian party Worldviews to their liking.

The Need for Four New Political Terms. Both Liberal and Conservative talk show hosts demonize people as being Liberal or Conservative. They do so because controversy increases ratings. Labeling and demonizing makes for a conversation with an "us versus them" confrontation: The "Good us"; the "Evil them". They use the terms 'Liberal' and 'Conservative' as implied expletives, often with additional adjectives in front to produce an implied redundancy in the expletive: Those crazy Liberals, Those stupid Conservatives, the immoral Liberals, the greedy

Conservatives – and on and on. The confusion and hostility surrounding the labels prevent the talk show hosts from carrying on rational discussions with Conservative Democrats or Liberal Republicans. Every individual that identifies themselves as such is quickly blown off as being mentally unstable by both the Liberal and Conservative talk show hosts.

This situation calls for new terms that are meaningful. The new terms will need to clearly identify the Worldview the individual embraces and the three Worldviews they oppose. The new terms should not cause a knee-jerk rejection or anti-label admonishment.

Table 7-1 (Current Party Affiliated with Worldview) (PROPOSED PARTY MEMBER LABEL)		
Are People Inherently Good or Inherently Evil?	**Who is Ultimately Responsible for the Welfare of the Individual?**	
	Government	Individual
Inherently Good	*Democratic* **DEFENDERS**	*Libertarian* **ADVOCATES**
Inherently Evil	*Reform* **ENFORCERS**	*Republican* **CONTROLLERS**

New Terms. In Chapter 6, the Political Interrogatory determined Worldviews were each associated with one of four different political parties. The reader is encouraged to review the constitutions and by-laws of these parties and verify for themself that the relationship of the political parties to the Worldviews indicated is appropriate. Proposed in Table 7-1 and 7-2 are new terms that are intended to stimulate and support common sense conversations.

New Terms as Synonyms. The four bolded terms in Table 7-1, DEFENDERS, ADVOCATES, ENFORCERS and CONTROLLERS are offered as descriptive political synonyms (labels) representative of the mindset of each party's members. These synonyms identify a characteristic of the individual belonging to each party that the members of the party consider to be a positive characteristic. The synonyms also describe the characteristic of each party's members considered to be the most negative and offensive characteristic by the members of the other three parties. These terms are intended to be used as synonyms in the same way the term Liberal is used today to refer to a Democrat and Conservative is used to refer to a Republican.

| Table 7-2 |||
| Labels to Identify Party Members |||
Party	Worldview	Political Synonym
Reform	Conservative-Democrat	Enforcer
Democrat	Liberal-Democrat	Defender
Republican	Conservative-Republican	Controller
Libertarian	Liberal-Republican	Advocate

The Role of Government. The terms were not chosen trivially. These terms reflect the role each group believes government should play in society. The following limited, brief descriptions are based on the Worldview beliefs of each party.

The ENFORCERS believe the general public is inherently Evil and the government is Responsible for their welfare. Therefore:

1. The role of government is to regulate and control the conduct of individuals in society by creating laws and enforcing the letter of the law.
2. It is government's responsibility to provide for the welfare of the general public, and to implement programs and

solutions to society's problems whether the general public wants those programs and solutions or not.
3. Government uses whatever force is necessary to exercise its authority to live up to its responsibilities and perform its job.
4. Citizens are subservient to the government: The individual must obey the law.

The DEFENDERS believe that the general public is inherently Good and the government is Responsible for their welfare. Therefore:

1. The role of government is to provide choices for individuals that meet the specialized needs and desires of each identifiable group, to defend and protect the citizens by creating laws and programs, and to ensure that the intent of the law is obeyed.
2. It is government's responsibility to protect, defend, and provide for all individuals in society.
3. The government has the authority to use its judgment and to make decisions that are final, even when such decisions involve the individual's relationships with others.
4. The citizen is subservient to the government's decisions: The individual is only Responsible to obey the law.[14]

The CONTROLLERS believe the general public is basically Evil but each individual is ultimately Responsible for themself. Therefore:

1. The role of government is to control the conduct and decisions of individuals by creating sufficient guidelines and creating agencies that have the authority to implement and enforce the guidelines[15] to the letter of the law.
2. It is government's responsibility to ensure that the individual does not harm others and to ensure that the individual does not consume too much of society's resources.

3. The government can usurp whatever powers and authority is needed when creating and enforcing guidelines that solve society's problems.
4. The citizen is subservient to the government but only to the extent the citizen must conduct their activities within the guidelines established by government: The individual is responsible to stay within the boundaries of acceptable conduct set up by the law.

The ADVOCATES believe the general public is basically Good and each individual is Responsible for themself. Therefore:

1. The role of government is to empower the individual by providing information and by ensuring that the individual's rights are not impaired by the government or by another individual or group.
2. It is government's responsibility to ensure that resources and freedoms needed for life, liberty and pursuit of happiness are available to the individual and to insure that those resources are not squandered by the government or by other individuals.
3. Government can not freely exercise any power or usurp any power or right that is not expressly given to the government by the individual and the government's authority is restricted to enforcing the intent of the law.
4. The government is subservient to the individual in all matters of judgment and conduct, and government must use restraint and show respect in all matters: The government must not trample on the rights of the individual: the individual is Responsible for themself and the consequences of their actions.

Social Reform. To provide another example of how the terms proposed relate to the differences in beliefs between the four political groups, consider Table 7-3 which contains a brief summary of the role the government should play in stimulating and controlling social reforms.

Table 7-3
Government Approach to Social reform

Political Synonym (Worldview)	Approach
Enforcer (Conservative Democrat)	Government enforces a code of individual conduct and social reforms through the creation of laws and strict enforcement of those laws.
Defender (Liberal Democrat)	Government defends against unwanted social activities by creating laws, mandating their compliance, and imposing penalties for violations of the laws.
Controller (Conservative Republican)	Government controls individual conduct and social reform through the use of mandatory guidelines, with stiff penalties for violators of the guidelines (regulations, rules, codes, etc.)
Advocate (Liberal Republican)	Government advocates responsible individual conduct and social reform by creating incentives and managing Expectations; reparation of damage is the focus and goal when enforcing the law.

In table 7-3 the synonyms are used as verbs in the description. But, it is not the use of the synonym as a verb that is important, it is what follows. Specifically:

Enforcer   Social Reform occurs through the strict enforcement of law: The implication here is that there is no second chance for the Evil citizen that broke the letter of the law.

Defender   Social reform occurs through mandatory compliance and penalties: The implication is that despite an undesired decision or action, basically Good individuals, after paying a penalty, will be given a second chance.

Controller Social reform occurs through guidelines and penalties: The implication is that the Evil first time offenders will suffer penalties – unless of course, the guidelines do not apply to them.

Advocate   Social reform occurs through the use of incentives: When penalties are imposed they are for harming another, not for violating a law or regulation, and any penalty imposed always includes reparation of any damages caused.

Moderates. When there is a conflict between a person's Worldview and the political party's Worldview, most people will leave the party – Moderates don't leave! That is why not everyone fits the synonym mold proposed above. Those individuals that hold a Worldview that is different from the party's majority and who stay with the party anyway, they are the Moderates. Moderates exist in all parties. Individuals that are not Defenders (Liberal Democrat) exist in the Democratic party and individuals that are not Controllers (Conservative Republican) exist in the Republican party. It is difficult to identify Moderates in any party as a group because they don't show any more agreement amongst themselves than they do with the majority in the party. There is a reason this is so. Moderates in the Democratic party can adhere to any one of the three other Worldviews. The same is true for Moderates in the Republican party. If you acknowledge this fact you will soon recognize this fact to be true; and you will see three groups of Moderates in each party. Each group of Moderates will push a Worldview that resembles the Worldview held by one of the other three political parties.

Why Moderates Stay. Moderates choose to remain in their chosen party for a variety of reasons. The two primary reasons are: First, Moderates want to be involved in the political process of selecting candidates for office, and second, Moderates want to be candidates for office. For example, there are areas in the country where one party has successfully filled the majority of political offices for years, so membership in that party is perceived by the Moderate as the only way to be involved, and membership in the party is the only way to get elected. There are a few Moderates that naively believe their efforts and arguments will eventually result in the party changing its Worldview: 'Change from within' is their goal. These Moderates' actions and comments usually cause a wake of chaos and confusion to continuously ripple through the party's meetings. These Moderates will view the disarray as part of the process of change. The party will view it as internal dissention caused by personal ambition.

Moderates in the Smaller Parties. The smaller Libertarian and Reform parties are loaded with 'Moderates" mostly because these parties and their members are struggling to clarify their fundamental beliefs. That makes it easier for a Moderate to bamboozle the members into thinking they, the Moderate, is a loyal party member. So many individuals who do not share these smaller party's Worldview have joined these smaller parties that it is often difficult to recognize the commonality of the majority. The problem that both of these smaller parties face is that many of the Moderates joined the smaller parties just to take advantage of the enthusiasm of the new party and the low number of members. It is easier to get recognized in a small party than a large party. As long as no one is the wiser, Moderates can personally gain from their membership in a party that embraces a Worldview inconsistent with their own.

Warning. All parties should be aware of the fact that Moderates will cause havoc for their chosen party whenever they can. Inevitably and unavoidably Moderates gain notoriety as they

The Political Primer

willingly walk away from the publicly stated principles reflected by the Worldview of the party they joined. When they walk away from these principles they are recognized by all as being Moderate because they willingly sacrifice their principles – actually their party's principles and beliefs – for the sake of "….whatever …"!

The only difference between a person being a Moderate and being a Party Jumper is that the true Party Jumper makes a deal and then leaves the party they were first affiliated with. The true Party Jumper acknowledges to the world that their Worldview is now that of their new chosen party. The Moderate does not leave the party they physically affiliated with even though the party they affiliated with does not share the Moderate's Worldview. See Part 3 for further discussions about Party Jumpers and Moderates.

A Quick Check. As was mentioned above, the terms chosen for synonyms were chosen because they seem to define the characteristics of the individuals in each group. These terms not only carry an implication of being in favor of, or opposed to, a large role for government in society, but they also carry an overtone of concern about the populous being either Good or Evil. Try these terms on for yourself. Consider the following four statements. Which one of the following statements best describes how you feel about the role of government? Depending on your Worldview, some of these statements will seem too wishy-washy, others too harsh. Only one of these statements should be agreeable to you concerning the role of government and government's treatment of its citizens.

1) Government is responsible for its citizens: Government must create and <u>enforce</u> laws, address problems, create whatever program(s) it deems necessary, and implement solutions whether people want them or not.
2) Government is responsible for the welfare of its citizens: Government's responsibility is to create laws and provide solutions to society's problems that will <u>defend</u> the populace against all harm regardless of the source of danger.
3) The people are responsible for themselves: Government is responsible to provide guidelines in the form of rules, regulations, and codes and must create the agencies

needed to enforce those guidelines so the guidelines can properly <u>control</u> the decisions of individuals and control the interactions between people in society.
4) People are responsible for themself and their family: Government should <u>advocate</u> responsible individual conduct by making sure that adequate resources are available to the individual, empowering the individual to provide for themself, to implement their own solutions to problems, and to ensure their security.

Are you an Enforcer, Defender, Controller, or Advocate?

The Next Step. You now have a political tool in the form of two Political Interrogatories. Query yourself. Establish your basic Worldview. That Worldview is a Worldview that was adopted by one of four major political parties in the United States. Ask other individuals the two Political Interrogatories. If you do you will realize that fundamental differences or fundamental agreements exist between you and other people. This step is important because your Worldview will never be the blueprint for the structure of a society you want to live in until the people in control of society and the people responsible for creating solutions for society share your Worldview! And, you won't know whether anyone shares your Worldview until you ask yourself, and ask others, the Political Interrogatories.

What does it matter? How different can those solutions be? How different can the future world be? Check out the solutions for major and minor problems in society in Part 2.

The Politician's Prayer[16]

Lord, give me the courage to change those things I can change;
give me the patience to endure those things I can not change;
and, give me the wisdom to know the difference.

CHAPTER 8

THAT'S IT!

That's all there is to Politics. Politics is not just a very serious contest – it is war! The outcome of the battle will determine which of the four Worldviews becomes reality. What kind of society do you want to live in? It is that simple. It is your choice! You are the foot soldier.

Now the challenge. Is there any relevance to the simple view of politics that has been presented to you? As the saying goes, the proof is in the pudding. What you have been given in this Political Primer is a technique for viewing the world that is sort of like a technique for viewing Magic Eye® images. Some people just stare at Magic Eye® images for a while and suddenly they see the three dimensional image that previously was obscured to them. Some people put their nose very close to the Magic Eye® image and then slowly move the image away. Other people use the technique of grabbing the Magic Eye® image at the corners and move the image in and out as they stare through the image, as if looking at something off in the distance on the other side of the page. Others rock the image, moving one side in and the other out, as they stare at the image. As your mind tries to piece together the information your eyes are sending, what you may first observe is a broad streak like pattern in the image. With persistence one small section of the image will come into focus, and then, ultimately the entire image. Once the three dimensional image becomes visible you will be able to look around in the picture, looking at each 3-D item with ease. Everyone that has observed these three dimensional images will acknowledge that the image will be lost if you get distracted or lose your focus for any reason. Bringing an image into focus becomes easier each time you do so.

Mark E. Glogowski, Ph.D.

Using the Political Interrogatories as a tool, you will be able to bring politics into focus. The twist is that as you stare at Reality using your Worldview, you create your image of politics. Depending upon which Worldview you use, you see a different image of how the world is and how the world should be. To bring politics into sharp focus will require the use of all four Worldviews so that you can see the solutions (images) the Worldviews create. When you are satisfied with a solution that you created with your Worldview you will begin to understand how Worldviews change society depending upon the solution they create. With the three dimensional Worldview perspectives you can generate, the full impact of politics on your life will be realized. Then, as you begin to look around society, you will see the consequences of solutions that have been implemented.

Using the Political Gap Meter. Bits and pieces of the Political Gap Meter have been displayed on the previous page. The image on the back cover is the author's concept of a Political Gap Meter. To use the meter, ask yourself, "Do I view other people as being OK? Do I consider other people as being basically Good? If so, imagine your Reality arrow being pointed toward 'Good'. If not, imagine your Reality arrow being pointed toward 'Evil'. Then ask yourself, do you make the decisions about everything that impacts you, or do you find the government is actually making many, or all the decisions concerning your welfare. If you are making all the decision concerning yourself, your Reality arrow should be pointing toward the 'Individual'. If you feel or believe the government is making decisions you should be making, your reality arrow should be pointing toward the 'Government'.

Now consider how the world should be. Answer the two Political Interrogatories and mentally point your Worldview arrow in the right Direction: If you believe you should be taking care of yourself and your family, and not the government, consider your Worldview arrow to be pointing toward the 'Individual'. If not, consider your Worldview arrow to be pointing toward the 'Government'. Do the same for the second Political Interrogatory. In an ideal world, should the people around you, and the strangers you see on the street, be basically Good or basically Evil? Point

The Political Primer

the Worldview arrow in the appropriate Direction. If the Reality arrow and the Worldview arrow overlap, things are good for you. Reality is as it should be. There is no political Gap. If you have mentally imagined the two arrows to be pointing in different Directions, the difference is the political Gap. That political Gap will motivate you to get involved in politics.

PART TWO

APPLICATION OF THE FOUR WORLDVIEWS

(The Four Political Philosophies)

SOMETHING TO THINK ABOUT

This is a Reminder
that the truth will Glisten
for people that Ponder
for people that Listen
discover your Belief
just look Inside
you have Revelation
you have a Guide

CHAPTER 9

INTRODUCTION TO THE APPLICATION OF WORLDVIEWS

God gave you a mind so that you could think for yourself.
God gave you free will so that you could choose for yourself!

As the saying goes, 'Lets get down to the brass tacks' and take a look at how all this political theory is applied in reality. The primary objective of Part 2 is to demonstrate the application of the Worldviews derived from the Political Interrogatories. Societies differ greatly depending upon the Worldview used to create the solutions. Those solutions will cause some features to appear, some features to disappear, and most of the remaining features to shift their characteristics. In the next chapter a simple, common problem, bored kids in the summer, will be used to illustrate the relationships between Worldviews, Direction, Approach, structure of society, features of society, and characteristics of features. When you understand how all of these interrelate you will then have an understanding of what is meant politically by the term 'change'. When you understand what is meant politically by 'change' you will realize that you cause 'change' to occur and that you do so in the selection process – when you select the people who will be placed in positions of authority over society. One issue at a time, those individuals will choose solutions that will cause the features of society to rearrange. When those solutions are implemented, the political change that you selected and created will become visible.

Part 2 begins with an essay discussing the political Gap and why you will, or should, get involved in politics. It then presents an explanation of what is meant by the Structure of Society. It will then present several essays covering a variety of topics. The future of our society is being created one issue at a time, piece by piece, solution by solution. The goal of every political party is the creation of a society where everyone in society lives according to the Worldview of their political party. The essays in Part 2 will illustrate the four different Worldview choices society has for each problem and issue discussed. Those issues presented include 'the homeless', 'lifeguards on a beach', 'zoning codes related to lawn furniture', 'use of deadly force', 'judges', 'abortion', and 'illegal immigrants'. Several of the discussions contain comments concerning the actual action taken or elaborations on actions that could be taken if a single Worldview were pursued.

If society follows a single Worldview for a long enough period of time, society will create that Worldview's ultimate future society. The ultimate future society that will be created from each Worldview is the subject of the last two chapters of Part 2.

By the time you have finished reading Part 2, you will understand the relationship between Reality and Worldviews, why people are motivated to get involved in politics, the difference between the 'structure of society' and the 'features of society', and how the structure of society changes the features of society as each Worldview's solution is imposed.

CHAPTER 10

YOUR REALITY – YOUR WORLDVIEW

Why you get involved. If you do not notice or care about events going on in the political world, and everyone is acting pretty much the same as they always did – going to work, going to school, doing the same things for recreation, day after day – then for you, life is good. You do not suddenly become concerned when you believe there is nothing to be concerned about. Why get politically involved? Your Reality is fine. Nothing appears to be changing that will affect you or your family.

The difference between Reality and Worldview is continually emphasized in this Political Primer because people are motivated to act politically only when their 'Reality' is in conflict with their 'Worldview'. This phenomenon, that motivates you and others to become politically active, is slow to surface and frustratingly ineffective. When those in control of society are pursuing your Worldview, you become less motivated to be involved politically. After all, the world is becoming and is operating the way it should. It will not be until long after individuals that hold a Worldview different from yours have been placed in control of society that you will ever notice. Not until long after the wrong Worldview solutions have been pursued and implemented will you notice new features of society appearing and cherished features disappearing and other features becoming distorted beyond acceptance. Then and only then will you say, 'This should not be".

Politics will matter to you if and when the Reality of your world ceases to be what it should be and the world no longer seems to be functioning the way it should function. But, sometimes not even then will you become politically active! When many people consider society to be spinning out of control and becoming something that it should not be, they will still sit back and do nothing. They wait. They wait in the hope that someone, somewhere, will propose a solution that will be implemented and that society will then go back to being what it should be. They don't know when. They don't know who. But they wait none-the-less. There is always that possibility.

It will only be when reality is no longer tolerable, then and only then will some individuals be motivated enough to become involved in politics. But therein lies the problem. Politics is not just about selecting the individuals to be placed in charge of society to make change; politics is also about selecting individuals to be placed in charge of society to maintain its structure. If you are happy with the structure of society and you stop being politically active, who is going to support those candidates that want to continue to implement your Worldview? Not you. Not if you stopped caring about who is in the positions of authority over society. You may be ignoring that political detail, but assuredly other people are not. They are unhappy about the way society is structured and they want to change it. Those people will be politically active. They will gain control of society and society will change. You and other individuals like you, who are happy with the way society is working now, will not notice your reality change until after the current politically active individuals have succeeded in placing into the positions of control over society individuals who are not pursuing your Worldview. You will not notice, not until after solutions that you consider to be wrong solutions have been implemented, that the structure of society has changed. By the time you notice, new features of society will have appeared, others will have disappeared, and the rest will have become unacceptably distorted in order to accommodate the 'wrong' Worldview solutions. Those solutions will reinforce what you believe is the wrong structure for society and politicians will have created a society that you will not want to live in. By the time you become motivated to act it may be too late. In the past, when Reality became something that should not be because of the Worldview being imposed, many people took drastic action to change their Reality. Thus the quotes:

> *"Give me liberty or give me death."*[17]
>
> *"Live free or die: Death is not the worst of evils."*[18]

If you are not vigilant in the pursuit of leaders that share your Worldview, society will change. Society will become something that you believe it should not be — and it will change one issue at a time.

Participation in politics matters even if it is just to insure that the structure of society does not change.

The way you live is worth dieing for!

CHAPTER 11

CREATING THE STRUCTURE OF SOCIETY

Features of Society. To understand what is meant by the features of society, consider a simple problem:

Problem: In the summer, when kids do not have constructive activities they will become bored and often mischievous.
Solution: Encourage kids to play baseball during the summer.

A simple solution, but you need to have many features in society that will support the solution. For example, there must be a sufficient number of kids available to form a team; then you will need additional kids available to form an opposing team; then several teams to make a league so that the kids interest will be maintained all summer long; the parents have to have been raised in a culture where they are willing to let their children participate in baseball; there has to be a place where they can play (a baseball diamond); baseball equipment needs to be available (baseballs, bats, and mitts, safety equipment); there has to be transportation to and from the game; people must have sufficient leisure time in their lives to get to the ballpark and participate; and then there are a number of miscellaneous societal features that normally are not associated exclusively with baseball, such as food and drink, restroom facilities, arrangements for medical care, and more. All these are necessary features of society that must exist in order for the baseball team to be viable. These features can be arranged in a lot of different ways.

In general, in order to implement any solution to any problem, features must exist in society that can be rearranged to meet the needs of the solution. That is a given. If any features required to implement a solution are not present, they will have to be created before the solution can be implemented. For example, the solution proposed requires a baseball diamond to exist. If no baseball diamond exists, then that feature will have to be created before the solution can be implemented.

It is natural to consider the arrangement of features of society to be the structure of society, but politically, the features of society and their arrangement are not what is meant when referring to the 'political structure of society'. For simplicity, 'political structure of society' has been and will continue to be referred to simply as the 'structure of society'. A rearrangement of society's features, neither a simple rearrangement nor a dramatic rearrangement, will produce a change in the structure of society. If the structure of society is going to change it will change before any of the features of society will be rearranged. The structure of society and the features of society are interrelated, but they are not the same: It is important to understand and to appreciate the difference and to understand their interrelationship. [Note to reader. In the next chapter we will introduce briefly the concept of 'societal structure', which is a reference to the arrangement of the features. To help keep the two terms clearly defined, keep in mind that the 'structure of society' is determined prior to the design and implementation of a solution. the 'societal structure' is the consequence of the implementation of a solution.]

So, what is the difference between society's features and society's structure?

The Structure of Society. The structure of a society is nothing more than the Direction and the Approach that is set in place to implement solutions to society's problems. The structure of society is determined and set by the individuals placed in control of society. It is their Worldview. It is just that simple. Nothing elaborate. Nothing fancy. Nothing complicated. Just the Direction and Approach of the Worldview of those placed in control of society is the structure of society.

Here is why Direction and Approach are referred to as the structure of society: To implement the baseball solution to the summertime boredom of kids, you need to create the baseball team. But, there are a lot of decisions that need to be made. The

The Political Primer

first step has to be to determine who is going to be in charge of making the decisions. Is an individual going to make all the decisions? If so, then who? If a group of neighbors are going to make the decisions, then how are they going to be organized? Is the government going to make the decisions? Then which government or government agency? Deciding who is going to make the decisions is what is referred to as Direction. You can not implement any solution without first choosing a Direction. Are you, another individual, or a group of neighbors going to work together and pool resources, or are you going to ask a government or government agency to implement the solution? Which Direction are you going to go in? Once you have determined a Direction, the group you choose to make the decisions can start planning how to coordinate and reorganize the features of society to make it happen. You can begin to plan your solution.

Those individuals placed in control to make the decisions will determine which features are needed and which features are not needed in society, and they will begin to create the plans for implementation of the solution. Some needed features may not exist. Those will need to be created (for example, the baseball diamond). Other features may have to be eliminated (for example, kids playing video games six hours a day). The solution will create and reorganize many of the needed features of society. Creating features is where most people focus their attention. Creating features and changing features is the primary focus of any proposed budget. But, before the solution can be completed, one more part of the structure of society needs to be determined: The Approach.

Those individuals placed in control will determine the Approach: They will determine who is and who is not going to participate. Their Worldview's Approach will determine who will play: Will everyone be allowed to play, because all kids are basically Good; or just some kids, because while people are reluctant to call any kid 'Evil', let's face it, some kids essentially are Evil. Those kids that are too rowdy or mischievous would need to be controlled. Better if they were not allowed to play. Any team they were on would soon have a morale problem. Other kids have health and other concerns: too heavy, too thin, too old, too young, not punctual, not keeping up their grades (at summer school). There is an almost infinite number of excuses that would justify why these non-preferred kids should be kept from playing.

But the Approach does not stop there. Those individuals placed in control will set their Expectation concerning conduct. What will be their policies concerning misconduct? Are they going to punish, banish, or take retribution on a wrongdoer? Will they implement corrective behavioral measures? Provide for restitution? Permanently ban any wrongdoer? What will be their Approach to choosing and managing the human element of the team? Will they Approach personal problems from the perspective that kids are basically Good and deserve second chances (note the plural form of 'chance' was used)? Or, will they Approach the human management issue from the point of view that, for the sake of the remaining team they will use punishment of a wrongdoer as an example of why the other kids must behave? The Approach will be consistent with the Worldview of those that have been placed in control of the decision making process, and those individuals will create a policy consistent with their Worldview. Do they give a child a second, third, or fourth chance because they are basically Good and can change, or never a second chance because the child should have appreciated the opportunity given them.

When you choose an individual to be placed in a position of authority over society, those individuals have the authority to decided what both of these pillars of the structure of society will be: the Direction and the Approach. Both are necessary to implement the solution. When you have determined the Direction and Approach you want to base society on, you will finally be in a position to decide who should be in the position of authority to make the decisions. Once you have determined the Direction and Approach, then and only then will the qualifications of a person's experience be appropriate to consider. Surely, the person you choose should be competent, but the person you choose must hold to your chosen Direction and Approach, – your Worldview – or the solution implemented will soon become something that just should not be.

To recap, the features of society will change when the solution is implemented, but the structure of society is set when you choose the people to be placed in control of society to make the decisions. Whether the baseball team functions the way you believe it should function is dependant upon what you believe (your Worldview) and upon the Direction and Approach (Worldview) of those chosen to implement the solution. The same is true for society as a whole; whether society works the way it should work is dependant upon your Worldview and the Worldview of those placed in control of society.

The Political Parties and the Structure of Society. The goal of every political party is to place in positions of authority over society those individuals who share the political party's Worldview, with the specific objective being that, after solutions are implemented, the Reality of how things work will be how things should work according to the party's Worldview.

In the baseball example, the structure of society was determined when a decision was made concerning who would be in charge of making the decisions concerning the Direction and Approach. The decision was a political decision. It was a decision consistent in every way with the goal of a political party, i.e. to place individuals in control of society that share the party's Worldview. If the individuals chosen held the same Worldview as you, then the right people were chosen. You could be confident that once the baseball team is in place, the features of society will rearrange in accordance with the chosen structure for society and the team will work the way those that created the solution believed the team should work. It was their Worldview solution that was implemented.

Whether society works the way it should work and whether the right people are in the positions of power over society is your decision. You are responsible for maintaining the structure of society or creating change in that structure by your decision of who is going to be in control. You create change.

CHAPTER 12

HEALTH CARE

A Real World Problem changing the Structure of Society. In the last chapter we discussed how Direction and Approach establish the Structure of Society. In this chapter the health care issue is reviewed in order to show how Direction and Approach are currently being played against each other by politicians striving to implement their Worldviews.

The United States supposedly has the best health care system in the world and Americans as a group have the best access to the best health care of any country in the world. So, the problem is not Health Care. The problem is health care insurance. Health care is one of the few features of society that remains in the individual's realm of Responsibility. The individual makes the decision when to seek medical help. That decision is often dependant upon the individual's ability to pay for the medical care. They can pay either directly or through health care insurance. The individual's problem is that they may not have the means to pay directly and they may not have insurance that covers their medical needs.

Therein lies the true problem and it is not an insignificant problem. Many people do not have health care insurance. Some had health care insurance until premiums increased and could no longer afford the insurance coverage. The increasing premiums has caused many companies to drop health care insurance as part of their benefits package to employees. Individuals that have lost their jobs in the economic down turn not only lost their income, they lost their health care coverage too. The lack of health care insurance is a concern because this shift will cause a shift in the characteristics of another feature of society, the quality of the health care received. Eventually, the lack of health care insurance

Mark E. Glogowski, Ph.D.

coverage will cause a decline in the medical care provided in this country. Many providers will be forced out of business.

Features of society, such as health care professionals, hospitals, and pharmaceutical companies will continue to exist in society provided they are compensated for their expenses and services. After the 2010 Health Care bill is implemented these features will reflect the Worldview of the individuals who held the positions of authority over society when the solutions were designed. If those individuals did not hold the same Worldview as their predecessors, which they did not, then their Worldview solutions will alter these features of society when their solutions are implemented.

Before the Democrats' 2010 Obamacare health care bill was passed, the health care system that was in place was a product of the Liberal Republican and the Conservative Republican Worldviews. In their worldviews you made the decisions regarding your health care and you determined whether you would or would not have health care insurance. While some companies independently decided to offer health care insurance as a benefit to their workers, it remained up to you, the individual, to decide when and if you needed medical care. And, having made that decision, you had the responsibility to pay the bill. The 2010 Obamacare bill evidently was written by individuals that embraced the Liberal Democrat and Conservative Democrat Worldview and it was supported and passed by individuals that held Liberal Democrat and Conservative Democrat Worldviews. Their solution: The government will make the decisions; the government will pay the bill.

The Democrats and Republicans will battle over this issue for years: Their Worldviews are incompatible concerning the structure of society that should be created for the health care industry. The Direction of Obamacare is clearly Democrat: Government will make the decisions. The Approach to Obamacare is on the surface, Liberal Democrat: You have choices. But, the goal of Obamacare is actually to implement a Conservative Approach where you will have no choice concerning health care or health care insurance. You will have health care insurance – or you will pay a penalty that is sufficient to wish you did have health care insurance. This has already been decided: The government already decided. They will also decide what health care insurance plan you can purchase. Not initially. They decided you can currently keep whatever health care plan you have. At least you can keep it until the insurance company goes out of business. Then, you will have no choice – you will have to purchase a government approved health care plan. Of course, the government will allow you to choose to purchase any coverage you wish (wink, wink, ha-ha), and you can purchase as much health care coverage as you can afford (wink,wink, ha-ha). Why the "wink, wink, ha-ha"? Because, as you pay the higher premiums for as much coverage as you can afford, all that will happen is that you will be paying a higher premium for the same coverage – the same plan and coverage but under a different name. Under Obamacare the government will determine what coverage companies can offer, and they will all meet the same government standards. Any plan that deviates from the government norm will eventually be gone because, if the decisions are made by the individuals that created Obamacare, their Worldview structure for society will cause all other non-governmental plans to be banned. The government will make decisions concerning what will be covered and what will not be covered, and eventually everyone will be given access to the same medical care regardless of the plan you are in. The exception of course will be the special treatment given to government officials and workers.

Now the catch: The health care plan as written does not stipulate what you can and can not be treated for, or how much you might have to pay, or for that matter almost no details have been specified. That begs the question, why did an entire congress vote for this incomplete bill? Didn't they read it? Congress is not illiterate. The bill is 2,000 plus pages long and continually references other bills and regulations, making the bill a horrendous task to read and understand – nearly impossible for the average person. So if Congress could not read or could not understand the health care bill, and most of the details were missing, why was it passed?

As it turns out, Democrats did not need to read the bill to support it. To the Democrats there is a problem with the current structure of the Health Care system: The problem is not that people did not have health insurance, the problem was 'how it worked'. The current system has created a Reality that is not how the Democrats believe the world should work . . . Government should be making the decisions, not you. So, no! Democrats did not need to read the bill to support the bill. The Democrats supported the bill because all they needed to know was that the bill gave the government more control over a problem in society. Therefore, the bill did go in the 'right Direction' and the bill did take the decision making authority away from the individual. Democrats in droves supported the Obamacare bill.

Republican Opposition. Republicans opposed the bill for the same reason the Democrats supported it. The bill gives the government control over the entire health care industry and takes the Responsibility and decision making authority away from the individual. The Republicans should strive to repeal the entire health care bill because that is the only way to get rid of the required structure of society that implementation of the health care bill will establish. In January of 2011, you might have heard President Obama say that he will not agree to any changes to the health care bill other than 'tweaks that will lower costs or improve services'. Are costs or services even specified in the bill? Obama stated that he is open to suggestions, but he will oppose any changes to the bill that will change the structure of health care system that the Obamacare bill was intended to create. He will only entertain any numbers anyone wants to suggest – nothing structural.

Why did he take this position? Why is he so adamant? You know the reason: It is through the implementation of the health care bill that the structure of society will be reinforced. It doesn't matter whether Obamacare works or not. By 2014 Obamacare will have been implemented and the change in the structure of society will have become entrenched.

So, what can you expect from the Republicans? It would appear the Democrats understand the Republicans better than the Republicans understand themselves. The Democrats deliberately left the details out of the health care bill: The phrase 'To Be Determined" is rampant. 'To Be Determined' is the Approach, not the Direction. The Democrats have left the 'To Be Determined' to the Republicans because, after all, most of the Republicans in congress are Conservative Republicans, and Conservative Republicans are good at creating rules and regulations. They like doing that. To allow the Conservative Republicans to work on filling in the blanks is a compromise the Democrats willingly made – as they laugh into their shirtsleeves. Democrats understand that some Republicans will gleefully jump at the chance to modify this bill in the belief that they will positively impact the fate of their constituents. Here is the dilemma the Republicans face: If the Republicans are not true to their Conservative values and if they adopt a Liberal Approach to fill in the 'To Be Determined' clauses in the bill, creating a ton of choices, the Republicans will be performing the role of the Liberal Democrat. If the Republicans remain true to their Conservative values, they will change the bill from a Defender (Liberal Democrat) Worldview solution to an Enforcer (Conservative Democrat) Worldview solution: If the Republicans Conservatively fill in the 'To Be Determined' blanks the they will leave few choices for the individual and they will impose many government controls to prevent abuses in the health care systems. A Conservative Republican approach to filling in the 'To Be Determined' clauses will dramatically strengthen the role of government. (What idiots the Republicans will be if they do not see this to be true!)

For the Republicans to ever have a chance of building a structure for society that will create a Reality for society that Republicans want to live in, the Republicans have to sink their feet in concrete and not approve a single line of the 'To Be Determined'. The Republicans are going to have to ignore the barrage of PU statements that will be made that are intended to make people believe the Republicans are not concerned about the welfare of society.

CHAPTER 13

THE HOMELESS

The Structure of Society. As a last example of how a solution reinforces society's structure, let's tackle a problem that has been around for a long time – the homeless. What do you believe should be done about the homeless? Do you believe being homeless is a problem the government should solve with a government program? Should laws be created that prohibit the homeless from being on the street so they will not be visible to people who are just going about their daily lives? Would you want to create an incentive so that people independently volunteer to help the homeless? If a government program is to be the solution, would you want the solution to be in the form of a straight forward government handout or a government work program? If you want individuals to independently step forward and resolve the problem of the homeless, would you tweak the business climate to create jobs? Or, encourage more donations to non-profit organizations? Or, would you prefer that society was structured so that there would exist effective incentives to entice the homeless individual to solve their own problems?

As is the case when trying to come up with a solution for any problem, the first step is to pick a Direction. Who is going to make the decisions? The next step is to pick an Approach. Will your Approach be to create criteria to determine when an individual is entitled to receive help, such as criteria to validate their worthiness and neediness? Or, would you just give food, clothing, and shelter to anyone that showed up expressing a need?[19]

That some people are homeless and in need is a fact over which there is no disagreement. Often the homeless find themselves in a societal structure that impairs their ability to improve their conditions. (a 'societal' structure refers to the arrangement of features in society, it is not the 'structure of society') Conceivably, for some individuals who did not enjoy life when they were employed and theoretically more self sufficient, the social structure of their homeless life is desired by them. There are other homeless individuals that just like the freedom of 'riding under the radar'. Then there are homeless that truly do not desire to remain homeless. Those individuals would appreciate help.

Regardless of the reason for the cause of the homeless situation, disagreements exist concerning the implementation of solutions because every solution crafted to solve the homeless problem not only creates a societal structure around the homeless, solutions create a structure for society that the homeless, and everyone else, will have to live in. Take a look at two extreme examples of solutions to the homeless problem:

At one extreme: Allow the homeless to fend for themself. Give them every opportunity to be creative so they can solve their own problems. Allow the homeless individual to consider home to be any public place they find themself: Parks, forest areas, undeveloped lands, isolated areas in metropolitan centers . . .

At the other extreme: Government can round-up the homeless and put them in a 'homeless village' or even perhaps in jail.

There are benefits that can be derived from both of these solutions. In the first example, the homeless get total control over their actions and their future. In the latter solution the homeless would at least be provided with a good meal and have a roof over their head every day, and they would no longer be a potential menace.

There are all kinds of solutions that can be crafted between these two extremes: Determining which solution is to be implemented is at the heart of politics. Who will make the decision concerning the homeless and whether the homeless will have any choice is dependant upon the Worldview of those in control of society.

Worldviews are implemented one issue at a time. If a single Worldview dominates the process of creating and implementing solutions, the result will be the reorganization of the features of society where the entire Reality of society becomes 'how the world should work' based on that one Worldview. Each Worldview creates it own unique solutions for each problem. The following will illustrate some of the options based on Worldviews that might be used to address the issue of the homeless.

The **Enforcer's Worldview** (Conservative Democrat) would have the homeless be required to register with a government agency that would then provide care and oversight. If they are unwilling to register or fail to register, they would be rounded up and placed into a homeless village of some sort, or placed in jail.

The **Defender's Worldview** (Liberal Democrat) would require the homeless to seek help from one of the many government agencies. The government's job is to provide sufficient incentives and a variety of types of aid so that everyone's needs are taken care of.

The **Controller's Worldview** (Conservative Republican) would require the homeless to seek aid from a well regulated private charity. If they choose not to take advantage of those organizations, that is their choice. But, if they cause any problem in society they will be jailed.

The **Advocate's Worldview** (Liberal Republican) would allow the homeless to choose the lifestyle they desire, but if they needed help or desired to change their situation the Advocate would freely, willingly, and gladly provide financial aid directly to a homeless person on the street, or where ever they are found. The Advocate would donate as needed to non-profit agencies that offer free help the homeless.

Mark E. Glogowski, Ph.D.

The Advocate's Worldview, while the most visible on the street, has been the least represented in political circles. The Advocate's Worldview has been so frowned on by individuals holding the three other Worldviews that specific legislation has been enacted in some localities that dramatically limit the ability of the Advocate to implement their solutions. People adhering to the other three political Worldviews do not desire to live in a Reality where they can observe individuals giving money directly to the homeless. They have therefore made it illegal in many areas for a homeless person to approach another person in a street or on a sidewalk and ask for help. They have also passed laws in some areas that have made it illegal for a person to give money directly to a homeless person on the street. The dislike for the Advocate's solution and the justification for passing laws against the Advocate's solution is as follows:

Enforcer's view: It is not the individual's Responsibility to help out the homeless. The homeless are the problem of the government.

Defender's view: The individual that provides direct assistance to the homeless is preventing the government from performing its function, which includes determining the needs of the homeless and regulating the distribution of aid.

Controller's view: The individuals that provide direct assistance to the homeless are considered to be contributing to the delinquency of the homeless by rewarding the homeless with cash – which the homeless will probably spend on drugs and alcohol. The homeless are a feature of society. How society deals with that feature is determined by the structure of society.

CHAPTER 14

LIFEGUARDS ON A PRISTINE BEACH
An example of the application of Worldviews

After a child drowned at a public beach, the fate of the public beach became a political issue: The question for elected officials to decide was, "What should the city do with a two mile stretch of unprotected (no lifeguard) beach at which the child drowned?" The following are potential solutions created using each of the four Worldviews.

Enforcer (Conservative Democrat):
Direction: Government has Responsibility to care for the welfare of its citizens.
Approach: People are basically Evil.
Proposed Solution: Close the beach to the public. Do not provide lifeguards. Make it illegal to swim at that location and any location where there is no lifeguard.
Rational: It is not safe for people to swim at that beach. The death of the child demonstrates that the general public is careless and reckless. Parents do not properly supervise their kids. If left open to the public more people will die because kids will bring dangerous objects to the beach, such as tire inner tubes, rafts, water cannons and beach balls. It is best not to open the beach to such activity. Also, it is not economically feasible to provide lifeguards along the entire two mile stretch of beach. If a lifeguard station is open anywhere on the beach it would still be necessary to provide continuous patrols along the entire beach to ensure no one swims outside the life-guarded area, and then additional patrols would be needed to insure people do not swim when lifeguards are not on duty. The Enforcer would point out that the government already provides safe,

life-guarded swimming areas at other locations. People can go to the life-guarded areas if they want to swim in the lake.

The ultimate Enforcer solution: The public has no choice. No swimming at the beach.

Defender (Liberal Democrat)

Direction: Government has Responsibility to care for the welfare of its citizens.

Approach: People are basically Good.

Proposed Solution: Provide limited swimming facilities with lifeguards at one end of the beach and close off the other end of the beach.

Rational: By providing a restricted area for swimming the government is accommodating the public's desire to swim at that location. A life guarded area gives the public another choice of a place to swim. The government can monitor the area to ensure that the public does not use any flotation devices. Because it is not possible to identify a good swimmer from someone that can not swim, prohibiting such items will prevent non-swimmers from floating out into deeper water where they can fall off. So, no! No one should be allowed to use flotation devices. The government can also make sure there is no hazardous fooling around on the beach, such as kids wildly chasing beach balls and shooting each other with water pistols and water cannons. By allowing swimming only in the life-guarded areas, the government can justify prohibiting swimming in the non-life guarded areas, and the government will be able to restrict swimming times at the beach as desired, such as when no lifeguard is on duty.

The ultimate Defender's solution: The public has a choice: Swim in the protected areas when the beach is open so the government can protect them, or don't swim at that beach.

Controller (Conservative Republican)

Direction: Individuals are responsible for themself.

Approach: People are basically Evil.

Proposed Solution: Find a private sector commercial company to open a swimming facility at that location. If no private sector service company can be found, the government could create a public swimming facility at one end of the beach – with lifeguards – and post rules and regulations concerning age limits, times of use, activities permitted, and what may be carried on to the beach, strictly regulating and enforcing rules for individual conduct on the beach.

Rational: This solution provides a life-guarded beach with increased protection for those that want it, and provides regulations for those that choose to take a riskier course of action. By officially declaring that the remainder of the beach is open to the public the government can set guidelines for activities in the un-life-guarded areas and the government can post the regulations concerning the approved activities. Those regulations can restrict the use of flotation devices and other swimming gear if perceived to be a hazard to the swimmer. Such prohibited items might include inner tubes and water rafts which an individual with poor judgment might use and then go out too far into the lake, slip off, and then drown because they can not swim. Age limits can be placed on individuals who swim in the unprotected areas, such as no children under 21 years of age without their parents. Age limits will insure children and young adults, who typically as a group display poor judgment, stay in the life-guarded areas. Regulations can identify times when the beach is open and when it is closed. The possibilities for enforceable guidelines are endless.

The ultimate Controller's solution: The general public is provided with choices that include a protected swimming area and an unprotected swimming area, with the unprotected area posted with a set of guidelines to be enforced that control the actions of the public and protect the public from their own foolishness.

Advocate (Liberal Republican)

Direction: Individuals are responsible for themself.

Approach: People are basically Good.

Proposal: Leave the beach open and free of regulations. If the beach is deemed dangerous, at most post a sign that describes the danger and states that the beach is unprotected (no lifeguards).

Mark E. Glogowski, Ph.D.

If people know the area has no lifeguards and they still want to swim there, they should be allowed to do so.

Rational: By posting a sign with a notice that the beach has no lifeguards, people will be notified that they swim at their own risk and assume liability for themselves and their kids if they allow their kids to swim. The notice can further indicate the location of the nearest areas where lifeguards are provided. If people choose to swim at the beach, in all likelihood, their choice was based on the fact that there are no restrictions on what they could bring to the beach and to use in the water. They may be willing to risk the chance of drowning as a satisfactory exchange for the experience of freedom. After all, assuming risk is the consequence of assuming Responsibility for oneself. To the Advocate, risk of death is an acceptable consequence for the rights to enjoyment, convenience, and freedom (otherwise reworded and rearranged as life, liberty and the pursuit of happiness). Prohibiting swimming in un-life-guarded areas is equivalent to prohibiting activities such as mountain climbing, driving motorcycles, car racing, football . . . or any activity that at one time or another has resulted in death. An open unrestricted beach provides the individual with the ability to choose their activities and the items they wish to use in those activities. If the beach is left un-life-guarded and un-regulated, all of the other laws of society are still applicable. It is the individual's Responsibility to ensure their activities do not disrupt the activities of others at the beach. Police already have the authority to arrest offending individuals. Regulations mandating swimming be allowed only in life-guarded areas removes freedoms and enjoyment.

The ultimate Advocate's solution: Allow people to have complete freedom to enjoy the beach as nature provided it. The only government activity would be to provide information, notices of known hazards, and recommendations of precautions for the public to voluntarily follow – or ignore. The government can also provide information on life-guarded beach areas and times, should the individual desire such supervision.

CHAPTER 15

THE USE OF CUSHIONED LAWN FURNITURE

An Example of the Application of Worldviews

Political philosophy plays a dominant role in the creation of local zoning codes. Zoning codes were initially intended to protect individuals against their own ignorance. A good example would be building construction requirements that ensure buildings are designed to endure earthquakes, windstorms, and snow loads. The construction requirements that would need to be met to build a structure that would survive such events are not readily known by the average individual. By implementing enforceable zoning code standards, a local government can be assured that the information that is available is used to keep their citizens safe.

Zoning codes are now used for every conceivable reason: They regulate where people live, how they live, what activities are permitted, where those activities are allowed, etc. Recently, determining what type of furniture an individual could own and place on their property for their enjoyment became a topic for discussion at a local village board meeting: The mischievous behavior of college students resulted in lawn furniture being set on fire in a back yard. At the meeting it was revealed that at the end of the school year, when students leave to go home, lawn furniture, sofas and chairs become a problem. They contribute to the bulk of waste that must be picked up by the village, which in itself was not the problem. What became the problem is that some of the students discarded furniture at the curb for trash pick-up and after being placed on the curb it ended up in the street. This created a safety hazard. Some students just left the furniture in the side yard or back yard, which produced an attractive nuisance and an occasional fire. These incidents were deemed to be a problem. The village decided that cushioned lawn furniture was the problem needing a solution.

Four possible solutions can be derived from the political Worldviews.

Enforcer (Conservative Democrat):

Direction: Government has Responsibility to care for the welfare of its citizens.

Approach: People are basically Evil.

Premise: Government is Responsible; people are Evil.

Suggested solution: Prohibit the placement of cushioned furniture on the lawn at any time.

Rational: The poor judgment displayed by the students is justification for implementation of strong, harsh laws. The current anti-littering law can not be enforced because the devious activity always occurred when no authorities were around to stop the activities, and the enforcement that has occurred has not stopped the furniture and cushions from ending up in the street. By prohibiting the placement of cushioned lawn furniture on lawns, the lawn furniture would no longer be a problem.

Ideal solution: Pass a zoning ordinance that prohibits the use of cushioned lawn furniture in people's yards in the village. Further, limit the dates and times any furniture can be placed at the curb for garbage pick-up; heavily fine anyone that fails to abide by the new zoning ordinance

Defender (Liberal Democrat):

Direction: Government has Responsibility to care for the welfare of its citizens.

Approach: People are basically Good.

Premise: Government is Responsible; people are Good.

Suggested solution: Mandate that discarded furniture be placed at the curb for trash pick-up only on certain dates and specify that furniture may only be placed at the curb during daylight hours.

Rational: Government should not restrict the choices of the individual and should assume the responsibility of disposal of trash. A separate program should be implemented to pick up the furniture. The responsibility of proper disposal of the furniture can be transferred to the property owner by making it the property owner's responsibility to call to arrange for pick-up. That way the village would not have to rely on the transient student for proper disposal of the furniture.

Ideal solution: The government provides for pick-up of the furniture on certain dates; the cost of the village's pick-up service can be passed along to the property owner in the annual tax bill.

Controller (Conservative Republican):

Direction: Individuals are responsible for themself.

Approach: People are basically Evil.

Premise: The individual is Responsible: people are basically Evil.

Suggested solution: Strictly enforce litter laws, using increased patrols and increased fines and penalties; a new enforceable zoning code would be an acceptable addition to this solution.

Rational: There are laws in place that already regulate the proper disposal of waste materials. What is needed is increased law enforcement. Banning the use of cushions would be considered an extreme, but more economical step to implement. A new zoning code where compliance can be verified during daylight hours would make it easier to enforce.

Ideal solution: Impose tighter controls on refuse disposal with severe penalties on those individuals found to violate the current zoning codes.

Advocate (Liberal Republican):

Direction: Individuals are responsible for themself.

Approach: People are basically Good.

Premise: The individual is Responsible: people are basically Good.

Suggested solution: Encourage proper disposal of all unwanted items using incentives.

Rational: The Advocate is opposed to zoning codes. People have the right to be stupid but they do not have the right to harm others. Placing lawn furniture near the street in such a way that it becomes a traffic hazard is irresponsible. Since such activities seem to be happening consistently, the situation needs to be dealt with. Since the government has assumed responsibility for the trash, the government should implement a program to remove such items through voluntary programs with flexibility in disposal dates. Regulations that would prohibit harmless activities such as sitting on a cushioned chair in one's backyard is beyond comprehension: The problem is in the disposal of lawn furniture, not their use. Any regulation, if there must be some, should only address the impact of the improper disposal of such items – not their use.

Ideal solution: Incentives should be implemented that encouraged proper disposal of unwanted items.

Comment: Default Enforcer Worldview. The village that had a problem with lawn furniture has had a history of frowning on political parties participating in the election process. Consequently, candidates for village office generally are not affiliated with a political party and have not made their political preferences known. Those individuals that identify their political Worldview or political party affiliation rarely got elected. This village illustrates the phenomena that occurs when politics is dominated by issues and not by political Worldviews: The default Worldview to which the entire group succumbs is always the Enforcer (Conservative Democrat) Worldview. Therefore it is not surprising that cushioned lawn furniture and cushioned porch furniture were prohibited in the village by new zoning codes: Thousands of dollars of almost brand new cushioned lawn furniture were observed being delivered by the villagers to the village's garbage drop-off center the following month, not at one of the many charitable agency drop-off facilities.

CHAPTER 16

USE OF DEADLY FORCE BY PRIVATE CITIZENS

Gun ownership and the use of deadly force are issues rampant with emotion, especially right after an incident where an individual was shot and died. Here are the Worldview positions concerning ownership of weapons and the use of deadly force.

Enforcer (Conservative Democrat)
Direction: Government has Responsibility to care for the welfare of its citizens.
Approach: People are basically Evil.
Position: The function of the police is to protect the individual. All weapons are the property of the state. The use of deadly force by citizens is prohibited and is never justified.
Rational: The individual does not have the authority to restrain another, therefore the individual should never consider restraining a wrongdoer, even if the wrongdoer has broken into the individual's home and threatens the individual's family. The individual's only permitted action is to attempt to identify the intruder and call the police. If threatened, the homeowner and family should flee. They are authorized to use only the minimal amount of force necessary to escape. Apprehending the wrongdoer is the Responsibility of the police, not the individual, therefore there is no reason for individuals to own weapons or use deadly force. The government temporarily loans weapons to individuals for 'recreational' purposes but only under government supervision. Then the weapons are to be returned.

Mark E. Glogowski, Ph.D.

Defender (Liberal Democrat)

Direction: Government has Responsibility to care for the welfare of its citizens.

Approach: People are basically Good.

Position: Individuals may own weapons, but all weapons must be registered. Weapons may only be used for the purpose stated on the permit that was issued.

Rational: People should not own weapons; most people do not hunt. When an individual is permitted to own a weapon, a statement must be on file indicating the intended use of the weapon. Any use of the weapon other than what was stated on the permit is illegal. Regarding deadly force, it is prohibited: Even when an intruder enters a person's home, the individual must first call the police and give the police every opportunity to handle the situation. The individual may use only the level of force deemed sufficient to escape from the intruder. If a weapon is used with deadly force it must be demonstrated that it was the last resort, that the deadly force was used in the individual's home, that the individual or their family were prevented from leaving their home by the intruder and were first physically threatened with deadly force. There is no justification for the use of deadly force in any other situation.

Controller (Conservative Republican)

Direction: Individuals are responsible for themself.

Approach: People are basically Evil.

Position: Individuals have a right to own weapons. All weapons are registered.

Rational: Any weapon can be used for recreational purposes or for self defense, so all weapons should be registered. Anywhere and anytime that an individual or another person are threatened with deadly force, the use of deadly force for self defense is allowed. The individual may use deadly force anytime they or members of their families are physically threatened. Deadly force may be used if the intruder makes no effort to voluntarily leave, even when the intruder is not considered to create a potentially life threatening situation, because it is the individual's Responsibility to protect their family from all harm: An intruder in their home is clearly a physically threatening situation.

Advocate (Liberal Republican)
Direction: Individuals are responsible for themself.
Approach: People are basically Good.
Position: Individuals have the right to own and carry weapons. No registration is necessary.
Rational: Who is going to identify their intended use for a weapon as robbery, murder, or assault? Individuals should not be limited as to where they may take their weapons or when they can use their weapons. Deadly force is allowed whenever another individual's action threatens a person's life or property. When an intruder enters another individuals home without approval, and fails to provide a legal document prior to entry certifying their court ordered permission to enter, the homeowner is automatically considered justified in using deadly force, especially if the individual is asked to leave and refuses, no matter the status of the individual (criminal, friend, private investigator, police officer, . .

Something to Think About

Moses asked God to provide his people with guidance about how to live. God therefore inspired Moses to write down ten suggestions for a better life. We refer to these suggestions as the Ten Commandments. But, were they intended to be hard and fast, unbreakable rules? Are people supposed to just blindly obey these Ten Commandments? Are there conditions where men of Good Will are expected to violate the literal letter of the law as defined by the Ten Commandments? Were the Ten Commandments written so that people would not have to think for themself, or decide for themself?

The Ten Commandments, as specific as they are, are broad and vague. As written, were these Ten Commandments supposed to be followed to the letter of the law or to the intent of the law, or were they just a guide which would lead to a better life? Were they just a statement of the Expectations of the conduct of men of Good Will?

For example: "Thou shalt not kill". What does this actually mean?

Thou shall not kill anyone?

Thou shall not kill anything?

Thou shall not kill for any reason?

Who does this apply to?

Everyone?

Even those in authority?

What about to protect yourself or to protect another from being killed or harmed?

What about a government using the death penalty as punishment, as a deterrent, or simply as a tool to protect society?

Does the commandment really state, 'thou shalt not murder!"?

If so, what is the difference and how does it apply?

What the Ten Commandments are, and what they need to be, is dependant upon your Worldview.

CHAPTER 17

THE WORLDVIEW OF JUDGES

Illustration of two points regarding Worldviews.

First: For judicial candidates, it is important for you, the voter, to know what the Worldview of the judge is.
Second: The Worldview of the individual, even a judge, is important when they decide how to handle a problem.

Judges deal with people when there are conflicts to be resolved. They will seek solutions based on their Worldview Direction and Approach. Determining the Worldview of a candidate for a judicial position is therefore important if you intend to choose a judge that will support your Worldview. Determining the Worldview of a candidate is accomplished using the same two Political Interrogatories. The Direction a judicial candidate will set once in office is determined by the candidate's belief concerning who they believe is ultimately responsible for the welfare of the individual: The individual or the government. But, the second Political Interrogatory should be reworded to:

"Which is more important, the letter of the law or the intent of the law?"

If you identify a judicial candidate's Worldview, you should be able to predict with reasonable accuracy what, as a judge, the candidate's priority and preference will be for punishments to impose. Most people today would consider this impossible because they have observed judges 'making up their own mind' and imposing sentences that are inconsistent with the traditional labels of Liberal, Conservative, Democrat, and Republican.

Clearly, judges do not follow the philosophical beliefs identified by these political labels.

Consider an example of a resident of a city who was legally carrying a properly registered, concealed hand gun and observed a person robbing a store. The resident pulls out his hand gun and fires a shot in the air toward the ceiling in order to dramatically grab the attention of the robber. The intent of the resident was to implement a citizen's arrest and to restrain the individual from leaving until the police came, which he did. Consider this hypothetical incident now occurring in a city that has a law that prohibits the discharge of a firearm within the city limits. The robber may or may not have been arrested, but the citizen was arrested for having discharged a firearm within the city limits. How would a judge rule on this case? If we apply the traditional political labels to the judge's bias and extrapolate the judge's conduct, you will get a confusing array of potential responses.

- **A Liberal** judge might look at the intent of the law and dismiss the charge of illegally discharging a firearm because it was the intent of the individual to do good, which he did.
- **A Democrat** judge might not be so lenient and would be expected to more likely find the resident guilty of reckless endangerment (the bullet had to go somewhere) and obstruction of the duties of a police officer (the individual assumed responsibilities given to the police).
- **A Republican** judge might dismiss all charges and complement the individual for a job well done.
- **A Conservative** judge might praise the resident for an act of citizenship in arresting the robber, but would still find the resident guilty of illegally discharging a firearm because they broke a law when they fired the gun.

These relatively rational Expectations can cause you to believe there is no value to assigning political labels to judicial candidates. In the example given, if you consider a Democratic party judicial candidate, which voters are currently referring to as a "Liberal Democrat", your Expectation for the example given is that when the candidate becomes a judge the candidate will either dismiss the charges or charge the resident a with a violation of the law. And, your Expectation of a Republican party candidate, which voters are currently referring to as a "Conservative Republican", would be that when the candidate becomes a judge the candidate will either dismiss the charges or charge the resident with a violation of the law. The only conclusion you can come to, if you are considering judicial candidates, is that it really doesn't matter if they are Conservative Republicans or Liberal Democrats, they are just as unpredictable.

Take another look at the predictions in the above example. Did you notice that the action of the judge described was based on just one aspect of the judge's Worldview. The judges were determined by the political terms Democrat, Republican, Liberal, and Conservative,? The predicted performance of the judge was based only on the Approach (the Good resident protected his neighbor property, versus the Evil resident broke the law) or only on the Direction (the resident lived up to his Responsibility to protect himself and others, versus it was not the resident's Responsibility to perform the function of the police). The responses in the example focused only on one aspect of a judge's political classification using current terms, not on both aspects of the judge's Worldview.

Each judicial candidate will hold a Worldview of how things should be and will use their Worldview as their guide. If the candidate is elected to be a judge, there are situations that will impact the candidate's application of their Worldview: In some cases, judges are restricted by law and their oath of office as to what they can decide or what they can do. Some judicial candidates have succumbed to PU statements or experienced life altering events that have emotionally impacted their opinion on some issues. Those decisions affected by an emotionally induced bias will have nothing to do with the candidate's Worldview. Assuming the judicial candidate to be free of such adverse influence, the specific combination of Direction and Approach that a candidate would pursue as a judge is Worldview dependent. In the following paragraphs, Worldviews are identified using the political synonyms Enforcer, Defender, Controller, and

Mark E. Glogowski, Ph.D.

Advocate. The candidate's anticipated solution is projected for each Worldviews.

Enforcer (Conservative Democrat) This judicial candidate believes the government is ultimately responsible to enforce proper behavior in society and that people, who are basically Evil, never consider the adverse impact that their actions have on others. Thus, the Enforcer judge will assign definitive punishment, and they will readily utilize agencies that have the authority to restrict the individual's future activities. Their preferred punishment of choice accomplishes both goals, incarceration in the state's prison system. In an effort to deter others from committing the same crime, Enforcer judges will readily utilize the punishment of a criminal as an example. The judge will not provide choices to those found guilty and will be concerned about the individual stepping outside the laws of society. An Enforcer will freely give maximum penalties. Surprisingly, Enforcers will avoid levying the death penalty except in cases that involve the death of public officials, law enforcement agents, or emergency responders. Causing the death of a government employee is considered the most heinous crime against society. Government agencies are utilized to enforce penalties. Little blame will be placed on the individual (after all, the government is ultimately responsible). No matter the level of severity of crime, the Enforcer will have a tendency to maximize the criminal penalties and minimize civil penalties.

Defender (Liberal Democrat) This judicial candidate believes the government is ultimately responsible for the welfare of the individual and that people are inherently Good. The Defender judge believes the individual will usually make the right choice if given the opportunity, and that the individual will re-consider decisions once it is made known to them that they had unnecessarily harmed another person. A Defender judge will place individuals into programs where, with the government's help, the individual will learn how to live their lives properly. If the government program is not successful, the Defender judge will not blame the individual: The individual will be given a reprimand and will often then be set free. When the government program does not work, the Defender judge will set a goal to correct the flaws in the program so that the next individual placed in the improved program will benefit from the government's efforts. If the individual happens to be the same original (repeat) offender, so much the better; the government will have another chance of helping the individual – and hopefully more successfully. The Defender will tend to minimize both the criminal and the civil penalties imposed.

Controller (Conservative Republican) This judicial candidate will agonize over how much Responsibility the individual can or should bear because the individual is incapable of making right choices. In the Controller's mind, this concern is justified by the very fact that the individual wound up in court. The Controller believes it is the individual's Responsibility to take care of themself and to stay within society's guidelines. There will generally be somewhat less of a tendency to place the individual into the hands of state agencies or institutions, and thus less of a tendency to incarcerate than an Enforcer or Defender judge. The government's role is to lay out and enforce strict guidelines. The criminal will have few, if any, choices. When the Controller judge has options for punishment, punishments that do not require incarceration are the options that are utilized. Controller judges will place an increased dependency on parole, but will expect very tight reigns placed on individuals given parole. Controllers will readily utilize technologies that provide a modicum of freedom for the criminal as long as there are restraints. Such technologies include ankle bracelet warning devices that alert the police of an individual's activities and location. If an individual demonstrated a gross neglect of a restraint order, a Controller judge would not hesitate to remove all choices. Failure to stay within the guidelines would result in penalties being imposed: Incarceration is often utilized as the form of punishment when it is clear the individual deliberately made decisions that ignored society's guidelines. Because of the Conservative view that people are basically Evil, punishment is used as a deterrent to crime, not as a correctional device. A Controller judge will maximize both the criminal and the civil penalties related to a crime.

Advocate (Liberal Republican) This judicial candidate believes individuals are responsible for themself and their actions, and they believe the individual is capable of making right choices. This belief is based upon the fact that the people in society make good choices every day and the majority of them do not end up in court. The Advocate believes the options available to individuals on the "straight and narrow" were, in all likelihood, not options available to the individual that ends up in court. The Advocate judge will tend to levy judgments that include restitution and work related punishment such as community service. Advocate judges will offer choices and incentives to encourage individuals to develop experiences that will help them make acceptable choices in the future. They will pursue choices and projects that encourage individuals to seek to "pay back society" for their wrongful actions, specifically those harmed. Punishment in the form of incarceration is usually the last resort. Incarceration is a contradiction of the basic precepts of the Advocate's philosophy: Incarceration itself removes the need and ability to make choices and the act of incarceration removes the need for individuals to accept responsibility for their mistakes. The Advocate considers incarceration as a less desirable means of enforcing society's laws, and does not pursue incarceration as a form of punishment: The act of incarceration transfers to the state the Responsibility of mitigating the negative societal impact of an individual's mistake(s) and, to the incarcerated individual, their incarceration and time spent is considered by them to be their payment of the debt due to society and to their victims.

What might seem surprising is an Advocate judge's view of the Death penalty. In an Advocate judge's Worldview, judges have the Responsibility to protect society from violent individuals. As a result Advocate judges will not hesitate to impose capital punishment when an individual has demonstrated a gross disregard for others. This position is consistent with the Advocate judge's need to maintain the "integrity" of their Responsibility as a judge and the belief that individuals must be held responsible for their actions. The Advocate judge cannot allow an un-repentant, violent individual to threaten other members of society with violence, even if, or when, those members of society are also incarcerated.

Comments: The Worldview of Judges in pleadings. A judge has the opportunity to accept or dismiss charges levied against an individual. The closer the presentation of the prosecuting attorney's arguments come to the judge's Worldview, the more likely the charges will be upheld. The closer the pleading of the defense attorney comes to the political Worldview of the judge, the greater is the chance that the judge will dismiss the charges against the defendant. This is not a hard and fast rule because there are always mitigating circumstances. However, once the case is heard and a verdict given, judges can and do rely on their discretion when determining the punishment that will be imposed, and that discretion is guided almost exclusively by the political Worldview of the judge.

The reader is encouraged to read additional comments concerning the Worldview of judges in Part 3.

CHAPTER 18

ABORTION

The abortion issue is very contentious. People hold very strongly to just one of the four possible Worldviews, and they have difficulty understanding how anyone can justify adhering to any of the other three Worldviews on this issue. A commentary follows the descriptions of the Worldview beliefs. In the following descriptions, keep in mind that someone is going to make the decision whether an abortion is going to be allowed. The "Position" refers to the Worldview Direction and Approach expressed using the more commonly used terms that describe people as being Pro-Choice or Anti-Choice, Pro-Abortion or Anti-Abortion.

Enforcer (Conservative Democrat)
The Direction: Government is responsible.
The Approach: People are Evil.
Position: Pro-Abortion, Anti-Choice
Rational: To an Enforcer, if a woman wants an abortion, that's a good thing. It stands to reason, if a woman doesn't want to have a child and then the woman becomes responsible for raising a child she did not want, the child has a high probably of becoming a problem for society. It is the government's Responsibility to determine when a woman will be allowed, and when they will be not allowed, to have an abortion. Laws and regulations should clearly identify those conditions. Each individual must apply to have an abortion and the abortion must be sanctioned by a government agency. No abortion may occur unless approved by the proper agency.

Mark E. Glogowski, Ph.D.

Defender (Liberal Democrat)
The Direction: Government is Responsible.
The Approach: People are Good.
Position: Pro-Abortion, Pro-Choice.
Rational: To the Defender, who is generally ambivalent regarding the life of the child/fetus, if the child/fetus survives it will probably just become another problem for the government to deal with. Therefore, the Defender's position is that it is up to the individual to choose whether to have an abortion or not. The government should help individuals make that choice. If the individual chooses to have an abortion, the abortion should occur in an abortion clinic run by the government. If necessary, the abortion will be performed free of charge. If the woman does not choose to have an abortion they can get special aid as a single mother – providing of course there is no 'man' involved with the support or upbringing of the child.

Controller (Conservative Republican)
The Direction: Individuals are responsible for themself.
The Approach: People are Evil.
Position: Pro-life, Anti-Choice.
Rational: The Controller is pro-life and holds the view that hardships a woman must bear before and after childbirth is a burden of their own making which they must be made to endure. Very strict guidelines must define when abortions are allowed, which would be almost never. People make bad decisions all the time. Having an abortion is one of those bad decisions people make. Giving birth to a deformed or mentally challenged (physically retarded) child, having difficulties in one's personal life, and having financial difficulties are not a reasons to have an abortion. The only true situation where a Controller would consider an abortion to be appropriate is when the pregnancy poses a significant and serious risk to the life of the mother and the potential survival of the child/fetus is unlikely.

Advocate (Liberal Republican)
The Direction: Individuals are responsible for themself.

The Political Primer

The Approach: People are Good.
Position: Pro-life, Pro-Choice.
Rational: In spite of their personal pro-life convictions, Advocates believe it is the pregnant woman's right to decide whether to have an abortion or to carry the pregnancy full term. Advocates will honor that decision. Advocates often offer whatever assistance they can to help the individual choose to carry the pregnancy full term. Advocates also believe it is wrong for government to have forced the termination of the pregnancy to be defined as and synonymous with the termination of the life of the child/fetus. Advocates also believe that government should encourage the woman to carry the pregnancy full term by creating a structure in society that will rearrange the features of our society to ensure the best chances of survival of the child/fetus, rather than insuring that the abortion of the pregnancy means the death of the child/fetus.

Commentary on the Abortion Issue.

The purpose of this commentary is to illustrate how the features of society will change as Worldviews are implemented.

The abortion issue and the Reality surrounding this issue is complex. There are individuals that stand fast and true to their anti-abortion belief that abortion is wrong for any reason. There are other individuals just as avid in their pro-abortion belief that it is not wrong and that the individual should be allowed to have an abortion no matter the reason or for no reason at all. Between these two extremes are the positions defined by the Worldviews. If you believe you don't hold one of the Worldview positions described above, continue reading the following commentary. Then, re-read the four Worldviews again from your new perspective. You will find you do indeed hold one of these Worldviews.

Those old enough will remember the era prior to the legalization of abortions. It used to be absolutely disgraceful for a woman to have a child outside of marriage. It was also extremely difficult for a woman to raise a child on their own since single motherhood was taboo and society was structured exclusively around a man being in the household. It is still difficult for a woman to raise a child as a single parent[20], and probably always will be.

Before the 1960's women died having abortions. Society, with its double standard, turned its back on such women for centuries: Being a single mother was shameful; but having an abortion was a crime. In the late 1950's and early 1960's, teenagers that were pregnant were often whisked away, never to be seen again by their high school friends. Doctors were prevented from performing abortions in medical facilities, so abortions always happened out of sight: In back alleys, in illegal clinics, in a foreign country. Sometimes, too ashamed to even tell her family, the woman would take desperate measures herself to abort the pregnancy. This usually resulted in serious injury, and without proper medical attention, often death.

Then society finally stepped up to the plate and put an end to the slaughter of pregnant women that was occurring in the United States: The U.S. Supreme Court Roe versus Wade decision came into effect. With abortions now being legal, doctors terminated pregnancies openly in hospitals and at their offices.

This created a new problem for society, but those in government wanted no part of the new problem. Most of the women who did not want the burden of the pregnancy also did not want the Responsibility of raising the child. Babies were being delivered – alive! Society turned its back. There were no funds to support these children; there was no mechanism to support them. There was not even a mechanism for adoption: If the mother did not want the child and if the doctor terminated the pregnancy, the government made it the doctor's financial responsibility to care for the child – apparently forever! Those in government chose not to rearrange features of our society where the child could be immediately adopted. The government chose to not even alter society's features so the child could eventually be adopted. And, those in government chose not to provide government financial assistance for the newly delivered child. The government made abortions legal but after that, as far as the government was concerned, it was apathetic; it did not care The mother, the doctor, and the baby were on their own. CBS ran specials featuring abortion issues during their supper hour Evening News. They showed newly born babies sitting on shelves, dieing from lack of care because nurses were prohibited to give them care – not even water. One episode showed the infant being drowned in a bucket of water, as if it were some pesky animal to be rid of so it wouldn't have to be dealt with again. There was an outrage from the public.

The fact that the new structure for society created by the new feature (the Roe vs Wade decision) created a new problem in society that was ignored by government officials. It didn't take long for doctors to find a solution to their problem. They invented ways to make sure the fetus was dead before it came out of the mother's womb. Saline injections worked, but the process was slow. Faster, more effective methods were created. Abortion was no longer just the termination of a pregnancy. It was redefined by doctors to be the termination of the life of the fetus. Today, if a pregnant woman chooses to terminate her pregnancy early it means the death of the fetus. Because of the way society has been structured using the Defender's Worldview, and because that solution did not include a role for other individuals to assume Responsibility, the Defender's solution completely ignored a feature of society (adoption). To make the Defender's solution work they just redefined a feature of society to accommodate society's new structure: They redefined the term 'abortion'.

The debate concerning abortions has now taken another twist. It would seem all of society has put on blinders. You can not discuss the original issue, which was the desire of the woman to terminate her pregnancy. The entire debate is now wrapped up in a theological debate: When does life start? When is a fetus a person? When is a fetus entitled to the 'rights of citizenship', and therefore government protection? The debate has expanded to the question, "When does life start?" At one extreme is the opinion 'the second a man's sperm enters a woman's egg'. At the other extreme is the view, not until 'after a normal childbirth', where a normal childbirth is defined as a natural birth or a C-section.

In their wisdom, those in government in New York State weighed in on this issue. They determined that, in New York State at least, a fetus becomes a child worthy of the government's

Mark E. Glogowski, Ph.D.

attention and protection at 24 weeks of gestation. Not earlier than that. Definitely not at 23 weeks. Consider a real case in New York State described in an editorial article written by Suzanne Schnittman[21]. She discussed the case of an individual charged with second degree manslaughter because his reckless driving caused the death of an unborn child whose mother was 23 weeks pregnant. But as it turns out, the mother had a C section after the accident. So when is a fetus a person? The letter of New York State law is clear, 24 weeks is the time period after which a fetus has achieved a lifespan worthy of rights and after which time every effort must be taken to save the life of the fetus/child. According to New York State, the 23 week old fetus, despite the fact that it was alive, is not a person requiring protection. The fetus was a government recognized non-entity! Never-the-less, in this case the child was placed on life support anyway and it was believed to be in a stable condition. Caring for the child was expensive. Had the mother been in the 24th week of gestation or further along, the state would have mandated the child's care, regardless of expense. The law specifies that when a child is 24 weeks or older the doctors are obliged to take every measure to save the child's life. At week 24 there would be no decision to make. But the mother was only in the 23rd week. The decision was made to terminate life support. The child survived more than two hours after being pulled from life support. So the question is, if the fetus/child was not a life that deserved protection from the state, can someone be charged with manslaughter? And if someone is charged with manslaughter, who should be charged? The fetus/child clearly died <u>after</u> being taken off life support – two hours after being taken off life support! Admittedly extreme measures were taken to save the child's life after the accident – a C section and life support – but the life was saved. Extreme measures are often taken to save a life after an accident, and some accidents take months, if not years, for the victim to recover. The fact that the measures were extreme should not have played a role in the decision. The person that caused the accident created the situation that resulted in the need for other individuals to make a decision to continue life support or terminate life support. The person that caused the accident did not make the final decision to discontinue life support; the decision to remove life support directly and irrevocably caused the death of the child/fetus. So, should anyone be charged with murder or with manslaughter? Who? The person that caused the accident? The person that decided to terminate life support? New York State – because they wrote the law that allowed the life support to be terminated for a 23 week old child/fetus? Or, no-one because the fetus/child was not yet a human life?

Regardless of the status of the child/fetus, the state in its wisdom found the person that caused the accident guilty of manslaughter for killing a child/fetus that the state does not recognize as a person worthy of protection!

While the above example is not truly tied to 'abortion', it is directly tied to the issue that causes the emotional blinders to be put on when people discuss abortion. Abortion has been redefined during the implementation of the Defender's solution to mean the death of the child/fetus prior to the termination of the pregnancy. If you hold a Worldview other than the Defender's, when it comes to the issue of abortion, your perception of the Reality of how the world works today is quite distant from your Worldview of how the world should work. You are experiencing a political Gap. Unless a new solution can be created and implemented that is patterned after a different Worldview, the changes that have occurred in the features of society will remain and you will have only one of two options: You can either be pro-abortion, or you can be pro-life. You either support abortions being carried out indiscriminately, or you oppose abortions for any reason. If you resolve to accept the Reality that was created to reflect the Defender's Worldview, you must embrace one of these two positions. It will be difficult for you to understand how or why people choose to believe there are other valid positions regarding the abortion issue. The pro- versus anti- abortion extremes have become the foundation of many irrational and emotional arguments.

From the Defender's point of view, when it comes to abortion, life is good. The world is as it should be. For everyone else, life is not good. There is a huge gap between Reality and the way the world should work when it comes to abortion.

Mark E. Glogowski, Ph.D.

In Search of a Solution. There are four different Worldview beliefs regarding abortion:

1. Pro-abortion and anti-choice
2. Pro-abortion and pro-choice
3. Pro-life and anti-choice
4. Pro-life and pro-choice

These four different Worldview beliefs, or positions, can not be equally implemented today because the current structure and arrangement of the features in society will not support the positions. These four Worldviews are based on fundamental principles of Direction and Approach. Thus when solutions are generated pursuing any one of these Worldview options, anything goes when it comes to developing a solution, including re-defining terms, re-arranging features, deleting features, and creating new features in society.

The issue of abortion should be an issue concerned with the termination of the pregnancy. A discussion that is needed never occurred: If you terminate the pregnancy, what is society going to do about fetuses that are being subjected to a shortened development cycle. Society needs to address this issue. It never did. It will only do so if abortion is redefined as the termination of a pregnancy. Once abortion is redefined we can consider the restructuring of the features of society to address the needs of the youngest of our citizens. This entire problem is one that relates to the establishment of Expectations: If the Expectation is that most people are basically Good, and the government were to take the position that all human life is to be cherished and saved, would not most women carry the pregnancy as far along as possible, many even full term, knowing that doing so would provide the best possible chance for their child to lead a normal life.

A Pro-Life Secular Argument. There is a secular reason why the government should take a Pro-Life, Pro-Choice stance, and why the government should never advocate or support abortions defined as the termination of life. It is well documented that, as the birth rate of a nation declines, the character of the society in that nation changes: A birth rate greater than the magic number (2.1 births per couple) is required to maintain the nature of a society. By splitting the abortion issue into the two original issues, and by defining abortion as the termination of the pregnancy, society could then address the issue of the care of the fetus/child aborted alive. The above descriptions of the four Worldviews would still hold for abortion defined as the termination of a pregnancy. Re-read them from the perspective that abortion now means the termination of the pregnancy and the fetus is delivered alive. You will find the rational pretty much still the same, but the second issue, what to do about supporting the fetus/child now needs to have its own solutions proposed and implemented in order to create and rearrange features in society sufficient to support that outcome and our newest and youngest citizens. This discussion is the topic of the next chapter, "Support for the Fetus/Child – An Extension of the Abortion Issue."

CHAPTER 19

SUPPORT FOR THE FETUS/CHILD.
An Extension of the Abortion Issue.

At the present time there is not an issue regarding women that had an abortion and kept their children – there are no children. However, if a different Worldview is pursued, there could be children that survive an abortion, and the women would again become single mothers. It may seem insensitive to call the new single mothers and the newly born children 'features of society', but that is what they are. Reflect back on the original example of the baseball team. Having enough children to form a team was a feature of society. So too, having children born alive as a result of an abortion (termination of a pregnancy) will be a feature of society. How the rest of society rearranges itself depends upon the solution implemented.

Let's assume society did redefine abortion to mean the termination of the pregnancy, not of the life of the fetus, and that the termination of the pregnancy could occur at any time. Let's also assume that society decided that human life begins when conception occurs and therefore regardless of when the termination of the pregnancy occurred, the best efforts possible will be made by society to save the fetus/child. It is believed doctors performing abortions, now defined as the termination of the pregnancy, would do what they did before the current solution was implemented: They would adopt procedures that maximized the chances of survival of both the mother and the child. It is believed there would be few, if any, exceptions. The following describe the Worldview solutions to how the mother and fetus/child would then be handled by society.

Mark E. Glogowski, Ph.D.

Enforcer (Conservative Democrat)

The Direction: Government is Responsible.

The Approach: People are Evil.

Position: Government assumes Responsibility and support for the child.

Rational: Because the government is responsible for the care of the child, and people are Evil, the government immediately assumes authority over the child once separation occurs and the pregnancy is terminated. The only exception is when a natural childbirth, c-section, or other special situations defined by law occurs. The government would establish agencies that would care for and raise the child.

Defender (Liberal Democrat)

The Direction: Government is Responsible.

The Approach: People are Good.

Position: Government programs are available into which the child is placed.

Rational: The government is responsible for the care of the child, and will provide several options for that care: One option is for the mother to raise the child. Government offers a wide range of support for this option. If the mother desires not to be responsible for the fetus/child she has the option of placing the child in a government run orphanage or placing the child up for adoption at a government operated adoption center.

Controller (Conservative Republican)

The Direction: People are Responsible.

The Approach: People are Evil.

Position: Strict guidelines for abortions exist with all rights concerning the child being forfeit.

Rational: Since terminating a pregnancy early is not healthy for the fetus/child, doing so demonstrates that the woman does not have the child's interest at heart. The woman would therefore forfeit all choices concerning the child's future. The child is immediately placed for adoption as soon as the pregnancy is terminated. Preferably, and whenever possible, the child is placed with a traditional married couple (man and woman).

Advocate (Liberal Republican)
The Direction: People Responsible.
The Approach: People are Good.
Position: Society provides incentives to carry the child full term.
Rational: Women are encouraged to carry the child full term rather than terminating the pregnancy early. The individual is given many options and choices concerning the raising of the child, including support from family, neighbors, friends and government. The structure of society allows the woman to choose to raise the child or put the child up for adoption.

CHAPTER 20

ILLEGAL IMMIGRANTS.

When you review these solutions, reflect on the fact that when these solutions are implemented the features of society will change, and as the features of society begin to change, the reality of what each individual will experience will become something that should, or should not, be. The Worldviews determine who will make the decisions and the approach that will be taken. The features of society are rearranged almost automatically to accommodate the solution. After all four Worldview solutions are presented, the Advocate's Worldview solution will be crafted for implementation for illustration purposes. Pay special attention to the way the features of society are projected to change as the Advocate's solution is implemented.

The Enforcer – Conservative Democrat.
The premise: Government is responsible for creating and enforcing a solution to the immigration problem; the illegal immigrants are individuals that are basically Evil.
Solution: Impose and enforce strict immigration quotas. Close the border. Put up barricades and impediments to prevent the illegals from crossing. Capture those that make it across and immediately deport them. If they get into society pursue them by any means. Prosecute anyone that gives illegals shelter the same as if the individual aided and abetted a known, proven, hardened criminal in the commission of a crime – because they did. Additionally, states that have been providing illegals money (welfare), health care, homes, and education, should be forced to stop such support. If necessary, have the federal government take over those state agencies if they do not comply.

Mark E. Glogowski, Ph.D.

The Defender – Liberal Democrat.

<u>The premise:</u> Government is responsible for creating and enforcing a solution to the problem; the illegal immigrants are individuals that are basically Good.

<u>Solution:</u> (This position defies logic, but it is the official position of many state and local governments across the US.) Enact strict immigration quota. Make any immigrant that was not government approved illegal. Put up barricades and impediments to slow, and hopefully prevent illegals from crossing the border. State and local governments are expected to provide the 'illegal immigrant', no matter how they made it into the United States, with whatever they need (driver licenses, welfare, medical care, education, . . .) If any individual is found providing an incentive to these individuals to make them want them to stay in the US, (such as employers), or found to be helping them to come into the United States (such as human smugglers) those individuals are to be punished. Periodically amnesties are granted to 'illegal' immigrants so that they can, en-mass, become citizens, which reduces the visibility of any problems that may be related to this immigration policy.

Controller – Conservative Republican

<u>The premise:</u> Illegal immigrants are individuals that are basically Evil people and therefore government is responsible for creating and enforcing a solution to the problem.

<u>Solution:</u> Close the border. Put up barricades and impediments to prevent the illegals from crossing. Place the military on the border. Capture those that make it across and immediately deport them. If they get into society, pursue them by any means. Create a new and more powerful regulatory agency that will enforce regulations affecting illegal immigrants. Prosecute any individual that provides illegal immigrants with food, clothing, shelter, or jobs. Also, force states to stop providing immigrants – legal or illegal – with money (welfare), health care, homes, and education.

Advocate – Liberal Republican

<u>The premise:</u> To immigrate is personal decision. Immigrants are basically Good people.

<u>Solution:</u> Change the immigration laws: All governments should have open borders. Create easier access to tourist visa's, provide work visa's freely, make citizenship more readily available and make it easier for a tourists to become part of the society they are visiting by encouraging citizens to help tourists become productive members of our society by providing them jobs and welcoming tourists as potential future citizens.

CHAPTER 21

IMPLEMENTING AN ADVOCATE'S SOLUTION TO ILLEGAL IMMIGRATION.

An illustration of how implementation of a solution will change society

Pursuing a hopeless dream with hope. The United States immigration policy has failed to create a Reality that anyone wants to live in. The individuals that have to deal with the issues created by this failed policy may not readily accept a solution created by the Advocate. The Advocate's solution begins with the belief that when an individual decides to leave their home country to come to the United States, the immigrant is a basically Good person that is seeking a better life. The Advocate's solution begins on the premise that every individual desires a chance to prove to the world that they are a Good person. They desire to become rich because that is the definition in our society of living the good life, but they also desire to do so by contributing to the betterment of society in a way that people will show their gratitude by making them rich. That is the American dream. Despite the seemingly hopelessness of their achieving their dreams under the current structure of the United States' immigration policy, foreigners continue to come into this country any way they can make it in, hoping that one day they will achieve their goal. Until then, the current structure of our society considers them to be nothing but criminals, no matter their background, their expertise, or their intent.

Implementing the Advocate's Solutions. Implementation of the Advocate's solution will change and even eliminate many real problems created by our current immigration policy. The reader is requested to withhold a knee-jerk reaction of rejecting the solution based on the Reality of how our country is currently

Mark E. Glogowski, Ph.D.

structured or on the existence of individuals with a criminal intent that will take advantage of the proposed solution during its implementation. This solution will create a new Reality, which is the intent of politics. Immigrants and immigration are features of society that will change to accommodate the new structure of society as the Advocate's solution is implemented. After you have comprehended the entire Worldview solution, then allow your initial knee-jerk reaction to surface, and modify your concerns as they might apply to the new Reality that will form. Your concerns will change. Some will grow. Some will shrink. Some will disappear. The problems of Reality will, in most cases, totally change character as the solution is implemented. For this solution, the only issue considered is the 'illegal immigrant'. Legal immigrants already have documents which allow them to reside in the United States.

An Advocate's Solution to Illegal Immigration. The following four steps are part of a solution that will change the current structure of our society regarding immigration. The features of society that will change are emphasized. It should be obvious to all that one of the greatest changes in society will be that of the Expectations that are established.

<u>Step One</u>. Stop calling the illegal immigrants 'immigrants', and stop calling them 'illegal'. They are visitors: They are tourists! A tourist is a person that has come into the country to visit for a period of time and has no legal standing as a resident or citizen! The United States has criteria for citizenship: You are born here or applied for citizenship (or your parents did). Some people have been given resident status while they are still citizens of another country. Those individuals have received a 'green card', work visa, or some other form of a long term stay visa. If an individual is not a citizen and is not a legal immigrant that has been issued a proper certificate authorizing a long term residency, then they are a tourist. They legally live elsewhere. That pretty much defines what a tourist is: someone passing through that legally holds or is entitled to residency elsewhere.

<u>Features of society that were changed by implementing Step One.</u> Look what happens because we take Step One, a little step that only requires a change of how we refer to the current 'illegal immigrants'. As a tourist they are welcome guests of our country. They are entitled to, and should be given, all the police protection any guest would expect from a host country. Clearly, when they are undocumented because they did not come across at an area where they could get tourist visa's, consider them tourists anyway. When those individuals are identified, why not just provide them with the proper short term visa? [Please relax and put your knee back down until you have reviewed the other features that change and the consequences. After you review the other three steps in the implementation of this solution you may find that indeed, this is a solution that will create a world that you would like to live in.]

<u>Step Two.</u> Open the borders and allow anyone with a sufficient amount of cash to support themself to stay for a period of time in the country as a tourist. For example, if the individual at the border indicates that they have $300, $600, or $900 (the actual amount is fairly irrelevant, but should be kept within the reach and needs of the average tourist) then the individual should be given a tourist visa that reflects their ability to provide for their needs while here. If they bring their family with them, the only requirement is that they have the means to provide for themself and their family while they are visiting.

<u>Features of society changed by implementing Step Two.</u> The current immigration policies are ineffective because they are failing to meet the needs of millions of people on all sides of this issue. With step 2, the number of border guards, currently a prominent, growing, and visibly intrusive feature of our society, could be dramatically reduced because the volume of people crossing the border 'illegally' will be reduced. The border wall itself, intended to keep foreigners out (and which could be instrumental under some Worldviews to keep citizens in), will be totally unnecessary.

Step Three. Have each tourist deposit $100 at the border when they come into the United States (again the exact amount is not critical for the solution to work). Tourists sometime become wayfarers. A wayfarer is a tourist that ran out of money and has no means to get back home. They are stranded in a foreign county. The tourist should be instructed to go to any government office at the end of their visa period and pick up a bus ticket back to the border. The ticket would be paid for by the deposit they left at the border. Alternatively they can pick up a refund for the deposit at the border at the end of their visa period. Individuals should be allowed to come back into the US at any time they can meet the monitory requirements for the Tourist Visa.

Features of society changed by implementing Step Three. Look what happens because of the Step Three: Individuals have a means to get home. By leaving and honoring the conditions of the Tourist Visa, immigrants create Good Will and because they are allowed to come back into the states after a reasonable period of time, the United States likewise creates Good Will among potential immigrants with honorable intentions. Such activity will reduce dramatically the difficulty of governing these (tourist) individuals.

Step Four. This step is the most important feature that will change because of the change in the structure of society. It is the feature that provides the characteristic of human dignity to our way of life again. Step Four is: During the period of time a person is visiting the United States on a Tourist Visa the individual is allowed to look for a job. If during that period the individual finds a job, the individual is allowed to take their employment/work documents to any Immigration and Naturalization Service office and receive work papers and/or a work visa that will allow them to set up a long term residency, even with the right to apply for citizenship. After all, if they are willing to work and are contributing positively to society, isn't that the definition of an individual that we want to have as a citizen? Our country is considered to be a melting pot because all people, regardless of their origin, have historically come to the United States, been welcomed, found a job, and became part of our society.

<u>Features of society changed by implementing Step Four.</u> Look what happens because of Step Four: There is a path to employment and to citizenship that is effectively non-existent today for every individual that today is considered an 'illegal immigrants'. This step will pretty much insure that every good intentioned immigrant will comply with Step Two and Step Three and obtain a Tourist Visa – and will return home if they fail to find a job in order to preserve their 'Good Will'. While initially the concerns that we already have millions of people out of work and that the tourists will take jobs away, consider also that we have millions of people on unemployment that won't take those jobs because they don't pay enough. There are individuals that live not more than a house or two away and others that live within commuting distance of a job who will not travel that short distance to accept the job. Then we have people that will give up their entire life in their homeland and travel thousands of miles to take the job that the person next door would not take. You can see pretty quickly the features of society that will change. Need I say more? Well yes, I do. There is the concern that wages will fall because of the onslaught of immigrants. Two features in society already act as a buffer. We have minimum wage laws. While the Advocate would consider such laws wrong, they are part of the features of our society none-the-less. This feature can be changed, and probably would be changed, to accommodate the implementation of the solution. But, most employers pay based on performance and abilities. This fact will not change much no matter the status of the employee. Every employer knows that, long term, you get what you pay for.

The end result of the Advocate's Worldview is that <u>all</u> people are treated with respect. And to the Advocate, that is the way the world should work

Comments: The Advocate's Views on Immigration. The United States did not have limits on immigration until the late 1800's. The borders were open and anyone that desired to come to the US to start a new life was welcome. Since the Continental Congress had a vote to make English the official

Mark E. Glogowski, Ph.D.

language of the country, the Expectation has always been that every immigrant would learn English as a part of their becoming a citizen. Historically, regardless of the country involved, immigrants have always had a hard time. In the United States, the group that came over last always pushed the previous group up the chain of acceptability and the last group in was saddled with everyone's prejudice.

When our government set immigration quotas and the need for official approval before an individual could immigrate to the United States, it did so because immigrants caused other features of society to be stressed and to change. Rather than to address those features of society, the government adopted the Worldview that the government must control, or at least regulate, immigration. Instead of being concerned because immigrants took the low paying jobs, the government concerned itself with the fact that its quota system did not meet the needs of other countries and immigration could not be controlled. The US government became concerned with the fact that many immigrants did not receive official permission to immigrate and therefore were illegally here, and therefore criminals. Illegal immigrants fear police – especially federal government agents. As a result, 'illegal' immigrants became the human resource pool for unscrupulous employers and for drug runners. After all, where are they going to go? If hardworking immigrants could be separated from the criminal element, and the honest, hard working immigrants were allowed to work in our country, the financial burden of dealing with the criminal element would be lessened. Clearly, the criminal element will still try to cross illegally; some might even try to sneak in as an honest person. Never-the-less, if honest, hardworking immigrants can walk across the border with a tourist visa, find a job, get working papers, and then apply for citizenship, a lot of our 'illegal immigrant' problems will disappear. For starters, there will be fewer individuals involved in illegal movement across the border.

Look at some of the other changes in the features of society that will change by implementing the Advocate's solution – changes that start simply with not automatically calling another individual that arrives from another country an immigrant.

The Political Primer

First, tourists would not be entitled to a driver license from any state. They should already have a driver license from their home country or they should go back home to get one. Tourists are not entitled to welfare. If they run out of money they should go back home: After all, they are tourists! If they followed Step Three, the tourists deposited funds at the border when they came in to the country. If they run out of money, they can get the bus fare that they left at the border with the Immigration and Naturalization Service (INS) and they will be able to go back home. They can always come back when they can afford to come back again – as a tourist. Tourists would be entitled to emergency medical care, but after that they would need to return home for further treatment. Tourists would not be entitled to an education or a mortgage to buy a home. They are tourists! Tourists are not entitled to welfare: They can either find a job and get work papers or go back home. This simplistic approach could solve a lot of financial problems for a lot of states: Consider California's financial problems! Implement the Advocate's solutions and California's financial problem is practically solved.

The added advantage to the Advocate's solution is that there will be a two million plus person tourist industry that will set up almost instantly, all of whom will have needs and desires. This tourist industry will immediately create jobs for many of those coming across the border, and will indirectly create numerous jobs and economic activity for other businesses that set about meeting the needs of the tourists.

CHAPTER 22

THE FUTURE SOCIETIES OF EACH OF THE FOUR WORLDVIEWS.

The structure that a society develops is dependant upon the Worldview that is being implemented. Those that govern society will always implement solutions to problems they believe are important to be resolved. But, if those in authority over society continue to utilize a single Worldview to create the solutions implemented, society will take on the unmistakable characteristics of the Worldview used to create the solutions. Eventually society will be completely dominated by the beliefs of a single Worldview. What will that society look like?

The following two sets of descriptions portray the features of each future society separately, based on the four Worldviews. The first set, in Chapter 23, describes what your political role in society will become as each Worldview is implemented. In the second set, Chapter 24, describes some of the features of a future society for each Worldview. It is recommended that when you start the second set, "The Future Features of Society as Determined by Each Worldview" that you go immediately to the description of the future society that would be developed for the Worldview that you believe you hold. Review that description of society. Ask yourself if this is the world you want to live in. Would you like to see this world created? If it is, good! Then review the descriptions of society that each of the other three Worldviews would produce. You will find that those three descriptions are truly descriptions of societies that you do not want to live in. However, if the description of the future society patterned after the Worldview you currently hold does not please you, and that description is a society you would not want to live in, then read the descriptions of the structure and features of society created by the other three

Worldviews and determine which of those descriptions represent the world you would desire to live in instead. If this is the case, and if one of the remaining three Worldview descriptions of society are more to your liking, then consider whether the Worldview you have chosen to support is truly the Worldview you want to continue to support.

CHAPTER 23

THE WORLDVIEW FUTURE POLITICAL ROLES OF THE INDIVIDUAL.

As society changes to reflect the Worldview of those in control of society, your political role in society will change. At the present time, in democratic countries, the individual is expected to participate in the process of selecting the individuals that will be placed in charge of society. If some Worldviews are successful, this right will be eliminated in the future. Worldviews have different requirements and will produce a different political role and Responsibility for the individual. The Worldview implemented will determine your political Responsibility, and it determines the when, the why, and the what of your involvement in politics. The allowed political activity you would experience is described below for each of the four Worldviews. The political feature for each Worldview's Ultimate Society is elaborated on a bit more in the next chapter.

Enforcer (Conservative Democrat):
Premise: Government is Responsible for the citizen's welfare; citizens are Evil.
Political Characteristics: Citizens have no political choice, authority, or Responsibility over who is in charge of society. The government has set in place a process for choosing candidates; there is usually only one candidate; and candidates always embrace the Enforcer's Worldview. Voting, if it occurs at all, will be a mandatory act of endorsement and a sign of allegiance.

Mark E. Glogowski, Ph.D.

Defender: (Liberal Democrat)

<u>Premise</u>: Government is Responsible for the citizen's welfare; citizens are Good.

<u>Political Characteristic</u>: The individual's political Responsibility is to select candidates from among the many candidates approved by government, all of which are required to display a psychological acceptance of the Defender Worldview.

Controller (Conservative Republican):

<u>Premise</u>: The individual is responsible for their own welfare; citizens are Evil.

<u>Political Characteristic</u>: Politics is an allowed activity but it is controlled. Individuals must meet a long list of requirements to become a candidate, including a psychological aptitude test that will guarantee the pursuit of the Controller's Worldview.

Advocate Liberal Republican:

<u>Premise:</u> The individual is responsible for their own welfare; citizens are Good.

<u>Political Characteristic:</u> A personal involvement in, and commitment to politics is necessary to maintain the structure of society. Being active in politics is considered good citizenship. Anyone can run for any position, but the emphasis on politics is always on personal Responsibility and respect.

CHAPTER 24

THE ULTIMATE SOCIETY.

Features of the Future Society of each of the Four Worldviews

The reader is encouraged to go directly to the description of the future society of the Worldview that they embrace: Enforcer, Defender, Controller, or Advocate. Read that Worldview description first and then determine if that is a society you would like to live in. Then read the other descriptions of the other future Worldview societies.

Mark E. Glogowski, Ph.D.

The Features of the Enforcer's Future World.
(Conservative Democrat)
The society the Reform Party is attempting to create.

If the government is totally controlled by Enforcers, and every solution to every problem is crafted by Enforcers, society will ultimately emulate the Enforcer's Worldview. It will be shaped around the belief that the government is Responsible for the welfare of the individual and that individuals are basically Evil. Government will have complete control over every aspect of society. The individual's entire life – their health, safety, welfare, housing, recreation, education and even their job – will be determined and managed by government agencies. Here are a few features of the Enforcer's ultimate future world.

Individual's needs: The individual's food, clothing and shelter is supplied to them by government agencies. The individual has very little choice. What choice they have is mostly limited to the mundane, such as which foods they eat and which clothing to wear, but they are limited by that provided at the government's "sustainable" food and clothing dispensary. The emphasis the government places on meeting the needs of the individual is only to insure the individual has the minimum provisions needed to meet their survival needs.

Education and Jobs: People are given an education and a job that a government agency deems appropriate. The education the individual receives is dependent upon a childhood assessment. The individual job assignment is dependant upon the individual's education and upon government's assessment of society's needs. There are no volunteer programs or non-profit agencies. Everything is mandated by the government and all tasks are government assigned.

Transportation: All modes of transportation are government owned. There is no individualized transportation with one exception: Government officials will get to use government owned vehicles for their personal use because of the importance of their positions and their responsibilities.

Recreation: At specified times, government run recreational facilities are made available to the individual.

Crime: Absolutely no wrong-doing (crime) is tolerated. The letter of the law is enforced. Punishment for wrong-doing is swift, severe, and excessive by today's standard. Recognizing that a percentage of the population is in constant opposition to the conditions government imposes (what would you expect from an Evil populous), electronic monitoring of individuals in both public and private places is common and extensive. Frequent and complete searches of individuals and of their property occur daily as a matter of routine.

Election Process: The government reviews the credentials and experience of potential candidates for public office. Each potential candidate must meet criteria established by the government to insure that they have the proper attitude (Worldview) for the position. One candidate is selected for each office. The populous then gets to vote for the candidate. Voting is mandatory and is effectively a pledge to obey the newly appointed member of the government (the ruling class). Non-voters are considered to be Evil individuals that object to the government run election process. Non-voters are placed on a suspect list and are heavily monitored because of the fear that they will try to change the structure of society that the government has established.

Commerce: All business and commerce is owned and controlled by the government. Private enterprise does not exist! The private sale of any item is prohibited. Government controls farming, manufacturing, and the distribution of all items in what are referred to as 'sustainable systems'. The distribution of every item is through a government distribution center. When an item is no longer wanted, it must be turned in to the proper government disposal center. Because there is no private enterprise, there is no banking system and therefore no need for money. The government determines what an individual can have and determines when an individual's consumption is considered to be excessive.

Class System: There is a real, permanent class system in society comprised of two groups: Those that govern, the elite, and those that are governed, the peasants. The lifestyles of these two groups of people differ greatly.

Money and the Economy: There is no need for money in an Enforcer's world because there is no free enterprise as we know it today. You fulfill your assigned service and receive the determined amount of government credits as a reward for your service. The credit may be spent for various approved items, such as food, clothing, and other material goods. You may purchase only a certain number of those items. There are no vendors of any type of service. Every service business has been absorbed into government agencies or has been determined to be unnecessary and banned. All personal services are banned, except for the elite. The individual immediately loses government credits when consumption is excessive.

Religions and Religious Beliefs: In the Enforcer's world, only one religion is allowed to be practiced, but that religion will either be an atheistic religion (there is no god, people worship the state) or a single monotheistic state religion where all variations of the religion are banned. In either case, if 'religious' practice occurs at all they will occur in government owned facilities. Whether religion is subservient to government or government is subservient to religion will be difficult to determine because those in government are considered to be religious leaders, or at least staunch followers of a religious leader.

Name of Enforcer's Ultimate Future World: Communistic Totalitarianism.

The Features of the Defender's Future Worldview.
(Liberal Democrat)
The society the Democratic Party is attempting to create.

If the government is totally controlled by Defenders, and every solution to every problem is crafted by Defenders, society will emulate the Defender's Worldview. Society will be shaped around the belief that the government is Responsible for the welfare of the individual and that individuals are basically Good. Government will create controls over society that will protect and defend members of society from harm. To a large extent, the individual's life – health, safety, welfare, housing, education and job – is predetermined and managed by government agencies. Here are a few features of the Defender's ultimate future world.

Individual's Needs: To meet their individual health, safety, and welfare needs, a variety of goods are made available at government distribution centers for individuals to choose from, but the individual's choices are monitored by the government 'sustainability' agencies. The government places much pride on insuring choices are available from which the individual may select.

Education and Jobs: An individual's education is free and provided by the government, but the individual's educational opportunities are determined by childhood exams. For employment the individual has many choices which include working at a government agency, regardless of profession, to volunteering to assist in one of the many government agency run 'good works' projects, which have replaced all of the non-profit and not-for-profit organizations.

Transportation: All transportation is owned and operated by the government. Exceptions exist, of course, for government officials and workers that received special authorization to use government owned vehicles for their personal use.

Recreation: For recreational activity, the individual can choose from any government approved activity programs offered at the government owned recreational sites. For public safety concerns all facilities are owned and operated by the government.

Mark E. Glogowski, Ph.D.

Crime: Wrong-doing is considered rare because wrongdoers are quickly apprehended and placed in an appropriately run government rehabilitation program available at government operated rehabilitation centers. The intent of the law is enforced. Punishment is minimal because when punishment is necessary the emphasis is placed on correction of behavioral patterns. Any conduct that negatively impacts or impairs a government function, such as failure to report to authorities that you witnessed another individual committing a crime, will result in excessively severe, harsh punishment. The punishment for impairing a government function is especially harsh when compared to the punishment levied for a crime that only caused harm to individuals or property. Monitoring of the populous is infrequent and considered unnecessary because people immediately report any wrongdoings to the authorities so that the wrongdoers can be dealt with. The most frequent crime reported and punished is the crime of acting independently without government approval or a permit.

Election Process: The election process is highly regulated with significant bureaucratic barriers in place for candidates to hurdle: Candidates first need to qualify for any position by first proving they are familiar with the government rules and regulations that pertain to the position, and then they must pass government mandated psychological exams: Their attitude toward government bureaucracy and government control (their Worldview) must be appropriate for the position into which they wish to be elected. This policy effectively ensures domination by a one Worldview order.

Commerce: Free private enterprise does not exist. Every business like endeavor must be pre-approved by the government and requires a permit. The output from every business is considered to be the property of the government. Government's emphasis is on providing numerous choices for the individual, thus the government instills a type of 'internal diversity competition' in the government's manufacture of goods. The government runs all distribution centers, manufacturing, and agricultural facilities.

Class System: A class system does exist, but the distinction between the governing elite and the governed peasant is not crisp and distinct: Everyone works for the government. Distinctions in the class system result from the graduated government merit system that is imposed on everyone. The higher up the internal government scale a person ascends, the more benefits they receive. Individuals move up based on such things as education, longevity on the job, the type of job, and of course, favors (equivalent today to 'brownie points' and 'who you know'.). Those individuals that get into a pubic office are immediately placed in the highest class of the merit system entitling them to the most benefits.

Money and the Economy: Workers perform a service for the government and receive a worker's benefit, which consists of a combination of welfare benefits (which can be applied to housing and food) and privileged benefits (credit to use for miscellaneous items and entertainment). There is no free market system. The credit earned can be used as desired, but only at government operated recreational facilities or at government run distribution centers. Spending habits are monitored to insure no one abuses their privileged benefits. Spending in excess on anything will result in a loss of privileged benefits (reduced pay).

Religion and Religious Beliefs: All religions have been belittled almost into oblivion. Those that believe in God are considered unstable and their beliefs have been equated to witchcraft, astrology, and stone-age humans worshiping fire.

Name of Defender's Ultimate Future World: Extreme Socialism.

Mark E. Glogowski, Ph.D.

The Features of the Controller's Future Worldview.
(Conservative Republican)
The society the Republican Party is attempting to create.

If the government is totally controlled by Controllers', and every solution to every problem is crafted by Controllers, society will emulate the Controller's Worldview. Society will be shaped around the belief that the individual is responsible for their own welfare and that individuals are basically Evil. Government will have created guidelines to completely control individuals. Within these guidelines individuals will be responsible for their decisions, actions, health, safety, and welfare. Government agencies will have been created to enforce regulations impacting every aspect of the individual's life. Other than being required to follow all the government's rules, regulations, and codes, a person can pretty much do and say and believe what ever they want. Here are a few features of the Controller's ultimate future world.

Individual's Needs: The individual is expected to work to provide for their own food, clothing, and shelter. Goods are manufactured or grown at government regulated manufacturing and agricultural facilities and are made available at government regulated retail outlets. When an individual needs aid and assistance, it is provided by highly regulated non-profit organizations.

Education and Jobs: Education is optional and is the Responsibility of the individual to pursue if so motivated. The choice of education and field of study is optional. Every job, regardless of profession, requires the worker to be permitted and licensed. Every individual must apply for and receive a proper license(s) and applicable permit(s) before applying for a desired job.

Transportation: Transportation is regulated. Licenses and permits to operate personal vehicles are available but limited to proven responsible individuals. Public transportation is the only transportation available to those that abuse the privilege of private transportation.

Recreation: Recreation is available at private but government regulated facilities.

Crime: To control the actions of individuals, the Government set laws in place as rigid guidelines for personal conduct. These guidelines are in the form of laws, zoning codes and agency regulations. Guidelines are rampant, widespread, and ubiquitous (everywhere affecting everything), and strictly enforced to the letter of the law. Punishment is determined by how much Responsibility the individual attempted to shirk. An offender is quickly apprehended and reprimanded, punished, or confined. Punishment is harsh, with little emphasis placed on correction of behavior.

Election Process: Strict regulations exist that control elections. Candidates must first be approved to run and they are made to follow certain general government guidelines for the desired job before they can be considered an official candidate for a position. Approved candidates must comply with all campaign laws and stay within the spending limits and campaign regulations that specify when, where, and how they may spend their time and money when campaigning. Candidates must also obey all other regulations and guidelines established by the government. The Evil populace is continuously attempting to infiltrate the government to change the government's Worldview. The regulations and guidelines are intended to prevent the Evil populace from being elected.

Commerce: Businesses are considered to be private enterprise but the government actually controls, through regulations, every business enterprise. Government actively participates in the ownership decisions of all businesses. Government regulatory agencies oversee every aspect of the economic system, without exception. A government seal of approval is required on every product certifying the manufacturer did not use unapproved raw materials or an unapproved vendor and that all of the government's regulations were followed during the production of the product.

Class System: A three tier class system exists: The elite elected to public office; the upper class that manage businesses; and the lower class peasant workers. The separation of the elite public official from the upper class manager is maintained by the elite using the undue power given to them as public officials and their ability to arbitrarily and indiscriminately impose new regulations on the business managers, including imposing limits on their productivity. Reduced productivity results in a loss of pay and privilege (see Money and the Economy). The separation of the 'rich' upper class from the lower class worker is strictly a class system created by wealth or the lack of it. With all the regulations in place, business managers have little control over the working class.

Money and the Economy: Money is an essential feature in the Controller's ultimate society. Individuals earn wages, set by government regulators. Those wages are in the form of cash and government sanctioned benefit coupons. Cash can be spent freely at a government regulated market. The benefit coupons are like food stamps and are restricted to the purchase of the items specified. The benefits, provided by the government, are funneled down from the government through the government's company run welfare office and distributed directly to both managers and working classes peasants. The process effectively makes every company an arm of the government's welfare agency. While the use of government benefits is restricted to items specified, the cash earned can be spent wherever the individual desires. The corporations' profits are limited by government. The government determines when and how much of a company's profit is excess profit and then confiscates the excess profit. Corporations distribute all the remaining profits to shareholders, of which the government is one of the shareholders.

Religion and Religious Beliefs: The government is ambivalent about religions; all religions are tolerated. But, all religions are subservient to the government: Every religion must be in agreement with the government's established rules and regulations. Religions are prohibited from teaching dissent, promoting individualistic ideas, encouraging individuals to independently act without government permission or government permit, or contrary to any established law, rule, or regulation.

Name of Controller's Ultimate Future World: Totalitarian-Authoritarianism

The Features of the Advocate's Future World.:
(Liberal Republican)
The society the Libertarian Party is trying to create.

If the government is totally controlled by Advocates, and every solution to every problem is crafted by Advocates, society will be shaped by the Advocate's Worldview. Society will be shaped around this belief: The individual is Responsible for their own welfare and people are basically Good. There is an Expectation of respect between people. Laws rarely need enforcement: Government regulations consist of guides and informational statements. Life, liberty and happiness are pursued in a responsible fashion, with the emphasis of 'responsible' being defined as producing no harm to another individual. Individuals are empowered to be fully responsible for themself. Here are a few features of the Advocate's ultimate future world.

Individual's Needs: Individuals work to provide for their own needs. Goods are readily available in a free market society. Any desired product can be manufactured or grown. When individuals are observed to be in need, people provide aid and assistance directly, even though many large, privately organized aid groups exist.

Education and Jobs: Individuals are responsible to pursue their own education based on their interest. It is up to industry to determine what job requirements must be met and it is business's responsibility to insure educational opportunities exist that are appropriate for the development of the skill set the business needs.

Transportation: Private vehicles are the primary mode of transportation. Public transportation does exist but it is operated by private enterprise; it operates effectively and economically and as a result it can compete against the cost and convenience of private transportation.

Recreation: Private recreational facilities abound everywhere. Each owner and facility has created their own rules and regulations for use.

Crime: The Expectation is that everyone respects the rights and property of others. When a wrong occurs, the intent of the law is enforced. Individuals make restitution for any harm done by their act(s). Only when necessary will government intervene. That happens when an individual's actions are deliberately harmful and the individual refuses to provide restitution; the government does not place an emphasis on punishment but rather on restitution and will cause the individual to bear full responsibility to mitigate the negative impact of their actions. Zoning laws and regulations are issued primarily for informational and advisory purposes, making the primary role of government that of being an advocate for proper conduct. As a consequence of that responsibility, governments provide free information on every conceivable topic known to the government, making the information freely available to everyone, thereby empowering everyone to make correct decisions.

Election Process: The election process is regulated only to the extent needed to prevent fraud, slander, and libel. The punishment is most severe for making a false accusation against any individual, including a candidate for public office. And, while a severe reprimand and chastisement may seem mild in today's world, in the Advocate's future world such a punishment is devastating to an individual. Candidates are allowed to advertise and spend without limits of time or money. There are no pre-qualifications to run for public office; the choice of selecting an individual for office is entirely up to the electorate.

Commerce: The economic system is the free enterprise system and it is very active. People make and sell what they want. Government barriers and involvement is almost non-existent. Government involvement in commerce is limited to the point of sale, where the government's focus is to ensure that individuals assume responsibility for the consequences of their private enterprise activities: While people can make and sell potentially hazardous products (cars, guns, etc.) they are not allowed to deliberately make and sell shoddy products, and they must provide sufficient information to the consumer to inform the consumer how to safely use their product. Government freely provides all information available to it to individuals and companies so that good decisions can be made by all. All company profits are distributed to the stockholders of the company: There are no corporate taxes.

Class System: There is no identifiable class system. Every benefit enjoyed by elected officials is enjoyed by everyone in society. The pay an elected official receives is, on the average, equal to the average pay of the average worker they represent. Differences in lifestyles that exist are caused exclusively by differences in individual wealth earned in the free market economic system.

Money and the Economy: There is no real estate tax, no income tax, and no corporate tax. All government services are provided free of charge, Local and state governments receive their revenue through a local sales tax (government's only point of interaction in commerce). The federal government receives its revenue through a tariff on imports of goods, services and raw materials (federal government's point of interaction in commerce). In the Advocate's world you can earn all the money (cash) you want and choose what ever you want to do with it. Free enterprise rules, as does respect for others!

Religion and Religious Beliefs: All religions are tolerated, regardless of whether they are monotheistic (one God), polytheistic (many gods), or atheistic (no god), provided the religion and religious leaders accept and live by the single mandatory principle of tolerance that states a person's belief in and practice of any religion is voluntary. No earthly punishment may be levied or threatened by government or any religion on an individual for believing, or practicing, or not believing or practicing any religion, with one exception: Religions that pursue control over government with the intent of eradicating the mandatory principle of tolerance. Every religion that requires a mandatory belief, practice, or membership, that encourages actual or threatened physical punishment against a 'non-believer' are considered to be terrorist organizations, not religions. Such organizations are not tolerated and are banned from society.

Name of Advocate's Ultimate Worldview: Liberty (Libertarianism)

PART 3

THE IMPACT OF WORLDVIEWS

Something to Think About

The Individual versus the Position.

One of the strangest happenings I observed at a public meeting was a public confrontation between two town officials. There was yelling and shouting. The public, observing the confrontation, was hotly divided on the issue and emotionally clinging to their views. The two town officials were the spokespersons for the two opposing groups. It was not a pleasant time for anyone at the meeting. When the meeting was over, the townsfolk went home, upset and still divided.

When the last of the general public left the room these two individuals, that were just moments before yelling and screaming at each other, began carried on in a friendly manner – joking around as if nothing ever happened. They even made arrangements to meet up at a local bar for a beer. I asked one of the individuals 'what gives? How can you calmly have a beer with someone that you were just screaming at?' The individual said, "I don't like the individual's political positions on most issues. Clearly I do not support his position on this issue. And, I clearly would prefer that he not hold the public office he holds. But, he is a good man and he is a good friend."

That is when I realized that in politics, as in life -

You may not like what a person does but you can still like the person.

The political lesson learned was, just because someone is highly qualified and is a nice, likable person, that does not mean they are the right person for the public office they are pursuing. Whether they are the right person depends exclusively on the Worldview they hold and the Worldview you hold.

CHAPTER 25

INTRODUCTION TO PART 3

In this section five topics have been selected to illustrate the impact the Worldview has on a person's beliefs. The intent of each essay is to further illustrate the concepts presented in Part 1 and to tie the resolutions of the problems each issue presents to the premise of the Political Primer: i.e., Politics is about implementing your Worldview. The following are brief descriptions of what is presented in each essay.

Chapter 26: The Moderate. Moderates are party members that are not pursuing the political party's Worldview. Moderates should be purged from your political party and should never be supported as a candidate.

Chapter 27: Beware the Party Jumpers. Party Jumpers are Moderates that will take personal advantage of the opportunity to jump to another party when the move is an advantage to them. They always jump to the detriment of the party they are leaving.

Chapter 28: Changing the Country for the Worst with One Catchy Slogan. PU statements come in all sizes and colors. One PU statement is very famous. Its use as a PU statement has been very effective.

Chapter 29: Judges. This is a continuation of the discussion on judges from Part 2, Chapter 17. A judge's Worldview will affect the way they approach solutions. This discussion focuses on what is involved in the implementation of a solution and how the pieces fit together. You may want to re-read Judges in Part 2 after reading this section.

Chapter 30: Interrelationship of Concepts. This chapter reviews and defines the concept of Worldviews, Expectation,

Mark E. Glogowski, Ph.D.

Responsibility, Change, Structure, Characteristics, Features, Problems and Solutions.

Chapter 31: Immigration – Illegal Immigration: The features, characteristics, structure, issues, problems, solutions, Responsibility, Expectation, and change. This is a continuation of the discussion concerning Illegal Immigration from Part 2, Chapter 21, but this essay brings together the concepts summarized in Chapter 30 and uses those concepts to define and illustrate the immigration problem. The immigration problem is complicated by a conundrum created by the application of a clever PU statement. After reading this essay, your perspective on this issue may change. By understanding the impact of Worldviews and the options available to society, you will have gained the best understanding of politics possible. You will have become politically astute!

The topic of immigration will be revisited again in Chapter 31.

CHAPTER 26

THE MODERATE

There are two uses of the term "moderate" in politics: One, to refer to a person that is politically Moderate, and the other, to refer to the individual that is fiscally moderate. In print they are distinguished by capitalizing the word when referring to a political Moderate. The political Moderate can be fiscally liberal, conservative, or moderate.

Many people equate being fiscally moderate with being Conservative. There is no relationship. Conservatives are often anything but fiscally moderate. Fiscal moderates have some common traits. They are usually quite reserved and usually wait for a proposal to be made. They usually also wait for a counter proposal, and then propose budgets and revenue allocations at a level of funding somewhere in between the two. They always support moderation of any proposed action: Not too fast. Not too slow. Not too much money. Not an insufficient amount of money. Don't be too stingy with resources. Don't waste resources. They are always in the middle, between the liberal and the conservative. Fiscal moderates are found in every organization, adhering to every political Worldview. They usually justify their proposals for moderation by stating, "All the facts are not available."

The word 'moderate' creates the image of a person that is rational, calm, and level headed, someone who will consider all of the facts before making a decision. The political term 'Moderate' would have you conger up an image of a person that is willing to set aside their personal convictions until all of the facts are collected and considered before making a decision. You expect a Moderate to be a person that strives to <u>not</u> be affiliated with the political left or right, nor any fanatic religious zealots,

Mark E. Glogowski, Ph.D.

nor environmental groups, nor labeled groups of any nature. Moderates want to be perceived as a person without bias.

Nice image, but hardly the reality of a Moderate. Moderates are always associated with and actively involved in political, religious, environmental, and other identifiable special interest groups. When decisions need to be made and the Moderate finally announces their decision, they become the center of attention. It is not because Moderates have special insight or access to secret caches of information. Almost without exception, when the Moderate's decision is finally revealed, all the facts needed to make the decision are not available. Their decision is clearly a judgment call. When information is lacking and the need arises, even a Moderate will not hesitate to make decisions without considering all the facts. Find a Moderate that does not agree with you and you will be the first to claim the Moderate is not being rational and that the Moderate is not considering all the facts.

Moderates are just like everyone else. They are members of organizations. They actively affiliate with special interest groups. They make decisions without considering all the facts. They are biased. They can be unreasonable.

Then what identifies a person as a Moderate? What makes them the center of attention? Wouldn't they be just like everyone else?

No. There is a difference. To identify a Moderate, and to understand what makes a person a Moderate, ask yourself this question:

> *"When and under what situation*
> *is a Moderate identified as being Moderate?"*

The answer: Moderates are identified when they perform their routine. That's right! Perform! They wait for the stage to be set, then once on stage, the Moderate is exposed for all to identify and observe.

What you first notice, and then for some reason just as quickly forget, is that Moderates are always physically, verbally, and philosophically associated with a political, religious, environmental, or special interest group's philosophy. Always! Political Moderates are always identified with a political party. They lead you and the public to believe they strongly hold the

The Political Primer

party's political Worldview. They work hard to be strongly identified with the party's Worldview philosophy so that people will recognize their "Moderate" nature when they take the stage. On stage Moderates indicate they are willing to compromise their Worldview beliefs. Moderates do not hide the risk they are taking: They could lose their 'good standing' in the political group they are affiliated with. They acknowledge the fact that their decision compromises the party's efforts to implement the party's Worldview. They want you to believe they agonized over the issue and when they finally made their decision, it was 'for the sake of expediency', 'for the better good', 'for public harmony', or some other meaningless, non-committal, altruistic, verbiage nonsense. Moderates reveal themselves by their willingness, for the sake of _____ (fill in the blank), to compromise and abandon their political Worldview beliefs, even though it is the Worldview beliefs of the very group they worked hard to be associated with.

Moderates are always sought out by the other side. When Bill Clinton wanted to gain support for his school programs, he sought out Republican "Moderates": Those individuals willing to abandon the Republican 'party-line' platform derived from the Republican's Worldview philosophy. Clinton sought support from the Republican Moderates that would compromise 'their beliefs' for the 'good of the country'. The advice for George W Bush, when seeking Democrat support for his tax cuts, was to strive to enlist Moderate Democrats, i.e., those Democrats that will walk away from the Democrat's party-line platform of no tax cuts.

Moderates are a liability to any party that supports their candidacy. During a campaign, Moderates consume not only the financial resources of the party, they consume the position on the ballot that should have gone to a stronger advocate of the party's Worldview. When a Moderate is elected the party becomes represented by an individual that is not committed to the fundamental Worldview of the party. The danger is that Moderates are unpredictable. When push comes to shove, Moderates will abandon the Worldview goals of those that elected them and they will not represent those voters. They will become individualists for their own personal reasons. When they can claim that they made their decision "for the sake of society", Moderates will side with any other group. Moderates will often initiate the process of compromise to gain personal recognition, and of course, any other benefits the Moderate can arrange for themself. When a Moderate is supported by a political party, the party looses a chance to support a true advocate for their Worldview.

In extreme cases, a political party can lose much more that just an advocate for their Worldview. Moderates may be dormant Party Jumpers that are just waiting for the right moment to jump.

CHAPTER 27

BEWARE THE PARTY JUMPERS

Party Jumpers are individuals that join a political party for reasons other than to pursue the party's Worldview. They are initially identified as being Moderate. They express opinions that conflict with the positions of other party members because their Worldview is different from that shared by the rest of the party members. Party Jumpers are always careful to justify their opposing opinions as an attempt to compromise or as an attempt to arrive at mutually agreeable solutions. Party Jumpers are leaches. They feed on the party's energy as the party's members pursue solutions based on their party's shared Worldview. Knowing that their opinions are controversial and not shared by the majority of the party's members, Party Jumpers still go through the effort to make sure their views on every issue is heard. The goal of the Party Jumper is to redirect the party's attention away from the solution derived from the party's shared Worldview. To the extent they succeed, even if all that they accomplish is to slow the party's progress toward implementing the party's solution, the Party Jumper will consider their efforts worthwhile. Party Jumpers become endorsed as the party's candidates when the party's members are duped and distracted with PU statements issued as political wisdom by the party's leaders and nominating committees

"You should support the most competent person".
"The individual paid their dues and put in their time. They deserve a chance at the position."
"The individual is a good vote getter."

Mark E. Glogowski, Ph.D.

Blah! Blah! Blah! The rest of the election cycle is spent trying to convince the party's members, and the public at large, that the chosen candidate is the 'best person qualified for the job'.

Party Jumpers are usually "competent", "qualified", "accomplished", "capable", "dedicated", and "hard working". They make ideal candidates because everyone likes them. But Party jumpers all share the same characteristics: Party Jumpers won't discuss their political Worldview beliefs: They subconsciously, at least, know they are seeking endorsement from a party that is pursuing a Worldview that they themself do not hold. Any discussion concerning political Worldviews would only emphasize that fact.

You may be saying to yourself that no one has ever discussed their Worldview beliefs as a candidate that you know of. That is part of the problem. The phrases "Worldview" and "Worldview belief" are not commonly used. In fact they are seldom used. Most People will freely talk about their vision for society, and their plans, and their goals, and their ideas for the future. But not Party Jumpers. Party Jumpers will only identify the issues that you are concerned about and they propose studies, committees, poles – any action that will make it appear as if they are concerned, but they will not reveal their Worldview.

Party Jumpers are always willing to compromise and find solutions where everyone can get along. When a Party Jumper is nominated to be candidate for the party, the Party Jumper has a problem. They have to avoid discussions that might reveal their true political Worldview beliefs and their problem is that any discussions on a controversial topic could result in their revealing their true political beliefs. To a Party Jumper, "A strong offense is a good defense." You are dealing with a Party Jumper when a candidate becomes contentious just because someone compared the Party Jumper's Worldview to the party's Worldview. The Party Jumper will immediately begin levying claims of negative campaigning, and hate speech, and complain of personal vendetta's being launched against them. Party Jumpers know they are seeking endorsement from the wrong party. Their only hope of succeeding in their effort to become the party's candidate is to be successful in distracting the party's members so they will not consider Worldviews. Party Jumpers leveling charges of negative campaigning by the opposition is usually only the first volley fired. Party Jumpers will do whatever it takes to keep the discussion off political Worldview solutions supported by the party's members.

No matter how prudent it might seem at the time to support a Party Jumper, the Party Jumper will always have an overall negative impact on the party. They should be weeded out by all parties. While "loyalty" tests are frowned upon as potentially subversive and reminiscent of McCarthyism[22,23], nevertheless, potential candidates should first be selected based on how well the individual's words, actions, and beliefs reflect the Worldview goals of the party. Loyalty to a party's Worldview is loyalty to the very fundamental purpose for which the party was created. The competency of the individual should never be the first criteria upon which a potential candidate is selected. A totally incompetent candidate working to implement the Worldview goal of the party is a far better person to try to get into office than the most competent, most qualified candidate that will work to create a society that is not based on the party's Worldview. Discussions concerning a candidate's Worldview beliefs should be the first discussion in every campaign – no matter how distasteful the candidate considers such discussions to be.

There are large negative impacts in store for the party that endorses a Party Jumper. The first large negative for the party occurs at the local level – the loss of the opportunity to endorse a candidate that strongly holds the party's Worldview. Then there is the loss of an opportunity to develop a person that would have eventually become a strong candidate that would have aggressively pursued the party's Worldview goals. Party Jumpers also drain the funds and energy away from the party. Their campaign message will not resonate with the Worldview beliefs of the party's members. The party's membership will begin to dwindle. If the Party Jumper is elected, the party's constituents will receive no representation and no chance of representation from this person because Party Jumpers are not pursuing the Party's Worldview. Once in office, the Party Jumper will be found to consistently vote against bills that reflect the party's Worldview. In many cases,

Mark E. Glogowski, Ph.D.

Party Jumpers are labeled "Moderates" because, 'for the good of society', they are willing to publicly compromise their publicly adopted Worldview goals.

When push comes to shove, and compromise is no longer an option, the Party jumper will acknowledge their mistaken party affiliation and they will change their political party affiliation. The consequences are usually dramatic. Such a case was experienced by the Republican party in 2001. Senator James Jeffers was a recognized Moderate in the Republican party and he changed his political party affiliation, leaving the Republican party – the party that supported his candidacy and got him elected – and enrolled in the Democratic party. The result of this action was that a Republican Moderate became a Party Jumper and the Republicans lost control of the U.S. Congress.

Beware of the Party Jumpers.

CHAPTER 28

CHANGING THE COUNTRY FOR THE WORST WITH ONE CATCHY SLOGAN

President John F Kennedy made this famous quote:
*"Ask not what your country can do for you.
Ask what you can do for your country."*

One day in November of 2000, Diane Ream, on her National Public Radio station (NPR) show, asked one of her guests to explain how the role of the federal government defined what America is. While the guest never really answered the question, the fact that Ms Ream asked the question illustrates an important phenomenon in the United States: When you think of your country you think of your government. For more than 150 years the representatives placed in power over society in the United States have been setting up your government to be responsible for not just the country's international affairs and national security. They have been changing the structure of your society to make it possible for your government to assume Responsibility for, and assume control over, every aspect of your American way of life — the economy, the environment, the welfare, the health, business, . . . even our personal safety when we travel. (You can't take that fingernail clipper on the airplane: You might cut yourself or use it to cut something or someone else!) In the Reality of those that have been governing our society for the past 150 years or more, the United States of America would not be the United States of America if it were not for the existence and power of the U.S. Government. When you think of your country today, you don't think of you, the individual. When you think of your country today, you think of the United States Government, federal agencies, federal laws, the national parks, . . . everything

Mark E. Glogowski, Ph.D.

that is government owned and government run. That is America. That is your country. Not you! When it comes to allegiance to your country, any negative statement about the United States' government is considered un-American. Over the past 150 years or more the government in the United became more than just the surrogate caretaker for the country. It became the country. The attitude of many individuals chosen to be placed in positions of authority over society is, 'what is good for the U.S. government is good for the country'. Kennedy's quote should have been more appropriately phrased:

"*Ask not what your <u>government</u> can do for you.*
Ask what you can do for your <u>government</u>."

Isn't that what Kennedy actually meant to say? Isn't that effectively the meaning of the original quote as it is interpreted today?

This rephrased quote reflects the change that has occurred in America. It reflects how service to your country has been distorted into the notion that, in order to serve your country you must serve your government. The Kennedy quote changed the attitude of many individuals. If you oppose the stated goals of those individuals given the authority to run our government, you are now considered unpatriotic. If I join you in your opposition, and we both agree the government is operating inconsistent with our desires, we are both unpatriotic. The Kennedy quote has been elevated by society to the level of a sacred mantra – interpreted as stated in the rephrased quote that if we are just working to provide food, clothing and shelter for ourselves and our family, we are not serving our country. Where in Kennedy's quote does the "we" fit that was referred to in the document that begins, "We, the people . . ." Where in Kennedy's quote is any concept, or even the implication of the idea that the individual is to be served by the government? Who works for whom? The concept that the government should serve us is there, but Kennedy's quote begins unconditionally with the statement that such a concept is wrong ! "ASK NOT . . .!" Who is the laborer? Who the master?

It is not the author's intention to be disrespectful to all those that were motivated to service by the original quote, but consider the real perturbation to our society that Kennedy's quote created.

If this modification of the original quote seems blasphemous, consider the following question:

Why should you not ask, 'What can my country do for me'?

That question is one of the questions we subconsciously ask ourselves every day. We answer that question every day when we walk out our front door, as free people, headed to do whatever we decided to do, go wherever we decided to go, and meet with whoever agreed to meet with us. That question is the one question that every immigrant has asked themselves before they made their decision to come to America.

What can America do for me?

What your country can do for you it does for every American. If no one cares what your country can do for you and no one else is concerned about what their country can do for them, then does anyone really care what happens to the country?

You should! You are the country!

Ask yourself, "What can my country do for me?" Then reflect on the fact that Kennedy's quote as originally worded obscures the greatness of this country. But don't stop there. Take a look at the original quote and tweak it some more. Use the quote as a tool to light the way to new discoveries and new understandings about your country.

It is not the answer that enlightens, but the question.

Consider the following format as a working version of the quote. It is offered as a means to motivate those individuals that are not motivated to guard their country against their own home grown tyranny. Insert your own appropriate term or terms in the blank spaces.

"Ask not what your x can do for you.
Ask what your x y doing z you."

Mark E. Glogowski, Ph.D.

For "_x_", use 'country', 'government', 'agency', 'school', 'union', any regulatory agency, or any form of authority
For "_y_", insert words such as "can", "is", "should be", and
For "_z_", substitute such words as "to", "with", "about", "against", "to promote", "to advance", "to stop", "to control", "to help" "to intimidate", "to protect", . . .

Use your imagination. Some substitutions will provoke emotions, some will provoke thought. If you pursue an answer to the question you created, you will need to reflect on your concept of Reality to determine what is practical and you will need to reflect on your Worldview in order to determine what is right.

Here is one example: "Ask not what your country can do for you. Ask what your country is doing to you."

Kind of tweaks your emotions a bit, doesn't it? You probably do not want to answer the question because subconsciously it makes you feel a bit unpatriotic. But, try anyway. Use your concepts of Reality and your Worldview: Make a Reality assessment of what you believe your country has done for you, how does the world work around you, and then ask yourself, what should be?

If the above format of the quote helps to stimulate both thought and emotion, then that is good! You will need both thought and emotion and a firm grasp on your Reality and your political Worldview when you realize what has happened in your country.

CHAPTER 29

JUDGES

Many people are of the opinion that campaigns for judges should be non-political, and that once in office, judges should act in a non-political manner. The consideration of judges being politically Liberal or Conservative does not seem to concern people. These labels are somehow acceptable. Liberal and Conservative deals only with Approach, with whether the 'letter of the law' or the 'intent of the law' is more important. Liberal and Conservative labels are promoted by the candidates and the press. The fear that a candidate being Liberal seems to generate is derived from the belief that Liberal judges will quickly release criminals because the Liberal judge places too much emphasis on the criminal's "redeeming social value" and not enough on the risk the criminal poses to society at large. The worst fear that a candidate for judge being labeled Conservative will generate is that, as a judge, the Conservative candidate will impose too strict of a sentence and will fill our jails with petty offenders. They will economically overburden society.

On the other hand, if you refer to a judge as a Democrat or Republican you will send a chill down the spine of most voters. These terms create visions of political bribes and crooked deals behind the closed doors of the judge's chambers. If voters don't have those fears, the so called non-partisan' watch-dog groups are willing to create those fears in your mind as they attempt to get you to support 'the most qualified' candidate – which by the way is the candidate that the watch-dog group has determined to be 'most qualified'.

For many years, so called "non-partisan" groups acted as review boards to certify that candidates are qualified to be a judge. They would review the background of judicial candidates and then rate them as 'not qualified', 'qualified', 'highly qualified' and some even 'most highly qualified'. The review boards stated intent is always to just inform voters so that competent candidates will be elected. Their goal is to make it impossible for someone 'not qualified' to be elected. Good intentioned legal associations (such as Lawyers Bar Associations) end up, in effect, controlling the election process by making it necessary for judicial candidates to become approved and labeled "qualified". There are two immediate problems to this arrangement: First, partisan politics still occurs, but it occurs out of sight of the voter and inside the organizations that conduct the reviews. The first response of the review committees and their parent organizations to such an allegation is that partisan politics does not occur inside the legal associations because the organizations were set up to be professional and non-partisan in nature. And besides, there is no mechanism for such political activities in the organizations.

That is the problem. There is no mechanism to make political activities visible. So, what is happening behind the scenes? Who actually controls these committees? Who makes sure a bias is not present and how do the organizations make that assurance? Who makes sure the political philosophies of the candidate are not considered if indeed they are not? Who insures that the Worldviews of the individuals doing the reviewing is not impacting their 'professional assessment'? You can not separate the person's Worldview from their opinions – not even on a professional level

The second problem with the non-partisan review boards is that, to the voter, the unstated implication when a person is declared to be 'not qualified' is that the 'not qualified' candidate is somehow corrupt and would become a menace to society and to the judicial system, if elected. When publicized, the rating of 'not qualified' from a review board is equivalent to legalized political liable and slander[24].

The first qualification of a judicial candidate that the voter should consider is whether the judicial candidate shares the voter's Worldview. A judicial position is important because the individual is given a position of authority over society. Judges enforce the structure of society by enforcing the laws created from solutions derived from that structure. If they did not enforce the laws they would effectively be creating a different Worldview structure. Judges have the power to force a structure on either or both parties in a legal dispute. Wouldn't it be better that an unqualified person as judge tried to create a structure for society that you wanted to live in, than to have a highly qualified person as judge easily succeed in creating a structure for society that you do not want to live in?

The current structure of society today has legal associations imposing rules and guidelines on judicial campaigns where those rules generally prevent a judicial candidate from disclosing their political affiliations and political Worldview. The result: You, the voter, do not have any knowledge of the single, most important piece of information about the candidate that you need – the Worldview the judicial candidate holds. The inability to disclose Worldviews and political affiliations leaves the voter without a clue concerning the Direction and Approach the candidates will take when they have to come up with solutions to problems in their court room. When judges have to come up with solutions they are not unlike other people. They too have to choose a Worldview, a Direction and Approach, to craft their solution(s). If during their campaign for office a judicial candidate cannot reveal their preferred Direction and Approach for society, how are you suppose to determine which candidate holds your Worldview? The current structure of political campaigns for judicial positions is designed to deliberately make you an un-informed voter!

This perturbation of the characteristics of our election process, in this author's opinion, is wrong. This should not be. Contrary to accepted opinion concerning judges, it is this author's opinion that judges should be made to identify their political philosophy – their complete political philosophy, not just their Approach to justice as a Liberal or a Conservative. Judges are required to intervene in the activities of society when there is a problem. For every problem a judge is faced with, just as for any other issue in society that any politician must grapple with, there are four different combinations of Direction and Approach that solutions can be derived from. The solutions that judges will implement is dependent upon the judge's Worldview. Depending on your Worldview, you will either agree or disagree with the judge's choice of solutions.

Mark E. Glogowski, Ph.D.

Two Examples of the importance of Judicial Candidate Worldviews

The Balance of this essay concerning judges is intended to reaffirm to you that when a person is running for a judgeship, their Worldview is just as important as the Worldview of any other candidate running for any other office. Even at the highest levels of judicial activity – the United States Supreme court, Worldviews play a major role in every decision. Do not vote for a judge that will create a world you do not want to live in. Do not vote for anyone that would have the power to appoint a judge if that person does not believe that the Worldview a judge holds is important.

A Judgeship Race for Family Court. In the late 1990's, during a local judgeship race in the Rochester, New York area, judicial candidates for family court were given the opportunity to make prepared statements that would then be broadcast by the local public radio station. In their statements they described basically the same, nondescript situations, with similar generic details surrounding the hypothetical cases. The responses concerning the solution each candidate would seek were interestingly very different. One candidate responded by focusing on the role of government. The other focused on the Responsibility of the plaintiff and defendant and the control each had over the situation The candidates drew from their personal political Worldview and revealed, in their answers, the Direction and Approach they believe most effective and therefore they would take if they were elected judge. The following reflects what the candidates stated was the proper role of a judge in family court: Clearly revealed is the difference between a Liberal Democrat's approach to judicially imposed solutions versus a Conservative Republican's approach to judicially imposed solutions.

The Democratic party's candidate, (party affiliation was revealed during the broadcast) responded to a hypothetical family problem and indicated that they[25] would seek out a government agency with an appropriate program into which they could place the individual and/or family. This candidate further elaborated, stating that if the program in which the individual or family was placed did not help the individual or family, the program would need to be evaluated and enhanced. The clear implication from the balance of this person's response was that it was important that government have the needed tools to aid individuals and families. If the program was not successful, but was subsequently reviewed and corrected, it could eventually be a useful tool. The next individual or family that needed to be placed in the program would benefit. The candidate indicated that they would work diligently with the government agency to insure the program was developed.

The Conservative-Republican candidate, (again, party affiliation was revealed during the broadcast as being Republican and the person was labeled as Conservative) described a similar situation. The candidate indicated that they would query the individual and family to determine what events were occurring in their lives that may be having a negative impact, then determine which situations the individual or family had control over, and what resources the family and individual had to work with. The candidate then indicated that the individual or family would be directed to address the situations using resources they had available. If the individual or family failed to resolve the problem the candidate indicated that they would then determine whether any government impediments existed that prevented the individual and family from successfully addressing their problems, and whether any non-profit or not-for-profit organizations could help. If all else failed, a determination would be made as to whether the individual or family needed additional assistance and of what type. The entire focus of the Republican candidate was on the individual's and the family's needs, their responsibilities, and their resources. There was not a single reference to a government agency or program except through the identification of "additional assistance" and "of what type" after everything else failed.

There was a real difference in the preferred Direction that the Democrat judicial candidate and the Republican judicial candidate desired to take the family: One emphasized government control and the other emphasized individual control.

The Presidential Bru-Ha-Ha. The fear of backroom partisan deals being made by judges stems from the fact that judges hold firmly to their Worldview Direction and Approach. Your not knowing what the judge's Worldview is does not mean that judges do not hold to a specific Worldview. They do. Judges, as a group, are individuals that hold true and do not waiver from their Worldviews. Remember the presidential elections of 2000. Voters had more than just a few little tingles of concern as the Secretary of State for the State of Florida, Nancy Harris, certified the votes in Florida during the Bush versus Gore battle for presidency. There was concern when the State Supreme Court of the State of Florida invalidated Harris' decision, and then when the United States Supreme Court upheld Harris' decision. Was this a case of partisan decisions being made behind the court room doors?

The presidential bru-ha-ha in Florida in the year 2000 is a good case upon which to reflect on the impact that political Worldviews have on judicial decisions. The decisions had the appearance of being the most negative form of partisanship – but that was not the case.

First, let's clarify the difference between a decision being partisan versus being political. There is a difference. If a decision is political, and is based on the individual's Worldview, the same decision would be made regardless of who benefits from the decision. If a decision is partisan, the decision would be made based on who would benefit. When considered from the point of view of the Worldviews of the individuals involved, the individuals made politically correct decisions. The judges' decisions and the decision by Ms Harris were consistent with the Worldview of the individual making the decision. Even though the decisions benefited a member of the party of the individual or group that was making the decision, the decisions were not partisan. Now lets elaborate a bit.

The presidential race was close. The fate of the nation rested on the official Florida presidential vote count: Would George W. Bush (Republican) or Albert Gore (Democrat) become president? The problem that came before the courts was, should the votes be recounted or should the certified count stand. The vote was certified by the Florida Secretary of State, Nancy Harris and certified several days after the elections. Ms Harris's certification was challenged in the Florida State Supreme court. The court ordered a recount. The U.S. Supreme court overturned the State Supreme Court decision and allowed the certified count to stand. Harris was a Republican. The Florida State Supreme Court was dominantly Democrat. The U.S. Supreme court was dominantly Republican. The vote count certified was in favor of the Republican candidate, George W. Bush. Knowing the Worldview of the State Supreme Court judges involved, it could be anticipated that the Florida State Supreme Court would choose to rule in favor of the manual recount and would set a new deadline for that count. Why? Not because Mr. Gore was a Democrat. It is because, as agents of the government, and being committed personally to the Democratic party's Worldview, the Democrat judicial members of any court, especially of a state Supreme Court, would feel totally justified to propose a government mandated solution for any problem they agreed to review. The majority on the State Supreme Court held the Worldview that the government is responsible for the welfare of the individual; in this case the whole country. It is inconceivable for anyone to believe that judges holding the Liberal Democrat Worldview would in good conscious deliberately restrict or prevent another government agency or organization from doing their job, including the Board of Elections. Therefore, in the minds of the Democrat State Supreme Court judges, a government review of the voting process is clearly better than having one individual certify the voting process and count. Party affiliation of the candidates and party affiliation of Ms Harris was not the issue in the minds of the State Supreme Court judges. The issue was whether an individual, even an individual authorized by the state as part of their job, can or should out rank an entire government organization or agency. Their answer was No. An individual, even an individual as an official of the state, is subservient to any larger state organization.

For similar reason it was inconceivable to believe that any Republican judicial member of any court, especially the US Supreme Court, would ever agree to a ruling that restricted the individual discretion of any elected or appointed government official when the official was exercising the authority given to them.

Mark E. Glogowski, Ph.D.

The members of both courts demonstrated their very strong conviction to their Worldview and the structure of society they want to build for the country. That very strong conviction was applied to the decision made by Florida's Secretary of State because her authority to exercise her discretion was granted to her by law. To a Republican judicial member of any court, it would be irrelevant whether the exercise of an official's authority and discretion, by any officer of government, curtailed the activity of a government agency or organization.

These decisions, made by the judges in each of the Supreme courts, were made in good conscience and they were made based upon the personal Worldview beliefs of the individual judges. Even though the judges in both courts appeared to be favoring their party's candidates in a partisan manner, the judges in both courts stuck to their political Worldview beliefs and did not compromise those beliefs in their decisions.

To make a point even clearer about the role of political Worldviews in judicial decisions, consider two hypothetical cases around the same event.

First hypothetical case. Consider the situation where the make up of the two Supreme Courts are the same, but the fate of the two presidential candidates were reversed: Bush was requesting the recount and Gore was opposing the recount. In this hypothetical case you have to overlook the fact that a person holding the Republican Worldview would rarely ever challenge the authority of a Secretary of State to make a decision they were entitled to make. But, for the sake of this hypothetical example, assume such was the case. It would be entirely consistent with the political beliefs of the Democrat controlled Florida State Supreme Court justices to have made the same ruling in favor of a manual recount for the reasons stated above. In fact, if they opposed a manual recount one would have a good argument that the judges were being partisan because they would not be following their Worldviews in their decision. Additionally, it would be entirely consistent with the political beliefs of the Republican controlled US Supreme Court justices to have made the same ruling in favor of upholding the decision of the Florida's Secretary of State even if that meant Gore was president. If the Republican controlled

United States Supreme Court judges considered making a different decision to support their party's candidate, the judges would have to compromise their political Worldview beliefs to do so. Most judges are individuals of very high integrity and, while they are willing to compromise on a lot of details, they are unwilling to compromise when it comes to the beliefs that motivated them in seek office and to stay in office – their Worldview. Judges rarely ignore their Worldviews in their decisions. That's Politics. When judges compromise their Worldviews and rule counter to their Worldview, that's Partisan.

Second hypothetical case. Consider the situation where the make up of the two Supreme Courts were different. Assume the Republicans had controlled the State Supreme Court and the Democrats controlled the US Supreme Court. Regardless of whether Bush or Gore had won, a Republican controlled State Supreme court would have supported Florida's Secretary of State Harris's certified vote count, because doing so would be consistent with their Worldview. It would not have mattered which candidate was requesting the recount. Ms Harris, as the Secretary of State of the State of Florida had the authority in her position to make the decision at her own discretion. Before a Republican dominated State Supreme Court would have accepted a challenge to the Secretary of State's authority to make the decision, an allegation of wrongdoing and significant evidence would need to be presented. If the US Supreme Court were made up of primarily Democrat judges and no contrary legal reasons existed, a Democrat controlled U.S. Supreme court would have ruled in favor of a state wide manual recount regardless of which side was the plaintiff. Again, in making such a decision the judges would be completely consistent with their political Worldviews concerning the role of government and the proper role of the individual. To do otherwise would be partisan.

Comments Concerning Judicial Candidates. The judicial candidate's Worldview is the most important fact that you can learn about any judicial candidate, including whether a judicial candidate has had experience or makes the 'qualified' list. Judges set precedent through their decisions. Each decision reached by a judge can be considered unique and cited as precedence in future court hearings. Since each decision made by a judge is based in part or entirely on the judge's personal political Worldview, that Worldview can have a dramatic impact on society. Voters should know the political Worldviews of judicial candidates. That knowledge gives voters all the insight they need to establish a realistic set of Expectations for any judicial candidate, and to be able to select a judge that will create a world that they want to live in. Only when it is necessary to choose between two candidates that hold the same Worldview beliefs would it be necessary to consider other criteria, such as being 'qualified' by a professional group. Since the typical voter has no means to determine the technical qualifications of judicial candidates, especially during their brief campaigns, there is some merit in having independent review boards.

Re-read Part 2 Chapter 17, The Worldview of Judges. What Worldview do you want used to enforce the structure of society?

CHAPTER 30

INTERRELATIONSHIP OF CONCEPTS

A number of concepts have been introduced and utilized in this political primer. It would be beneficial to review those concepts, firm up their definitions, and discuss how they interrelate before giving the final example of the application of Worldviews and their impact on politics and society.

The concepts that will be reviewed and defined here include:
Worldviews
Expectation
Responsibility
Change.Structure
Characteristics.Features
Problems.

Worldviews. Politics is about Worldviews – there are only four! They are created by the two Political Interrogatories. Worldviews are so closely related to the concepts of Expectation and Responsibility that it is difficult to say, off hand, without going back to the basics of Chapter 2 and the Survival Concepts discussions, whether a person's Worldview creates the person's Expectation and concept of Responsibility, or whether the person's Expectation and concept of Responsibility creates the person's Worldview. What is constant in society is that when political change occurs in society, the change occurs because those placed in control of society are pursuing a different Worldview.

Feature, Characteristic, Structure, and Change. These terms are defined as follows:

The term '<u>feature</u>' refers to the features of society. Features are the organizational or tangible elements of society, the presence or absence of which is required or the presence or absence of which makes the society unique. Some features are essential to the existence of society: For example, people, language, and government are essential features of society: Without people you don't have a society, without a language society can not function, and without government there would be no common code of conduct or mechanism for society to resolve disputes. Optional features of society would include such things as: The presence of utilities (electric lines, natural gas lines, sewer lines, roads), organizations (schools, retail outlets, manufacturers, religions, clubs), and any aspect of society that can be labeled that people could live without but the presence of which makes an impact on society.

Features of society all share this distinction: A feature is either present in society or a feature is absent from society. There is no middle ground. You either have a government, or you do not. You either have utilities, or you do not.

<u>Characteristics</u> are attributes of features of society. Features can have any number of characteristics. Characteristics of features do not change, they shift. The relationship between characteristics and features is best explained with an example. Consider 'people', a necessary feature of society. 'People' have many characteristics. Lets consider three: The first characteristics to consider is the number of people present. There will always be a number of people present because when the number is zero there is no society. So the characteristic of the feature 'people' referred to as 'number of people' can shift from two to billions. The 'number' of people present is one characteristic of the feature 'people'. Another characteristic of people is the 'average age'. While each person has a specific age, the feature 'people' in society can have a characteristic average age that is very low if a large number of children present in society, or very high if a large number of elderly people are present. There is never a time when the feature 'people' does not have an average age. Another characteristic of 'people' is gender. While there are only two genders, the characteristic of the feature 'people' can shift from all male or to all female. It is usually a mixture of both. In every case of the characteristics of a feature are always present but display themself on a scale that shifts.

The Political Primer

Every feature has characteristics. Government, a necessary feature in society, displays a characteristic that can be referred to as 'political leaning'. That characteristic of government can shift from Conservative Democrat, to Liberal Democrat to Conservative Republican to Liberal Republican and can be comprised of any mixture of these political leanings.

As the needs and desires of society are met, the characteristics of the features of society shift to accommodate the new features that were created. Shifts in the characteristics of the features of society reflect the needs that are required to be met as determined by the Worldview solutions being imposed on society. The features of society and the characteristics of those features create the Reality that you live in. When the characteristics of features become unacceptable, the shift in the characteristics of features are viewed as problems requiring a solution.

The structure of a society is the Worldview Direction and Approach of the people placed in control of society. The Direction and Approach selected to create solutions determines which features of society are needed, which features are allowed, and which features are prohibited. The 'structure' of society is reflected in the requirements created by the Direction and Approach concerning the features that must be present or absent. The structure of society is determined by you when you select and empower an individual by placing them in a position of control over society. The structure of society immediately becomes their Worldview's Direction and Approach.

The structure selected for society becomes visible when solutions to problems are implemented.

Political Change refers to the selection of a different Worldview Direction and Approach for the creation of solutions to society's problems. Political change occurs when new people are placed in control of society who have a different Worldview than that held by their predecessors. It is that simple. These individuals pursue solutions that agree with their Worldview Direction and Approach. That pursuit of a different Worldview Direction and Approach is what changed and it will ultimately end up visibly changing the features of society. As dramatic as the 'visible changes' in features of society may be, the appearance and disappearance of features of society, and the shift in the characteristics of features of society, they are merely symptoms indicating that a political change in society has occurred. The average citizen will observe the effects of political change, never recognizing the cause, and they will consider the effects observed to be the political change. True political change will induce a cascade effect on the Features and Characteristics of the features of society. This takes time. Political change, if it is going to occur, will occur immediately after an election: You will cause it to occur by selecting individuals that hold a different Worldview from their predecessors, and the change will occur immediately upon those individuals taking office.

Expectation and Responsibility. The concepts of Expectation and Responsibility play a major role in addressing society's needs. To illustrate this fact, consider the Responsibility a driver assumes when driving an automobile. Clearly, the driver assumes Responsibility. No one would ever claim government is Responsibility for the actions of a driver behind the wheel of a car. Government does, however create laws and rules of the road and governments restrict by law who can drive. But, once behind the wheel, the driver is in charge. The driver makes the decisions where they go, how fast they go, whether they go, even whether they will obey the laws and rules of the road established by governments. The driver is Responsible.

To maximize the 'convenience' of having an automobile, drivers on occasion wait until the very last minute before leaving to their destination; after all, when they leave is the driver's decision. Knowing that other drivers want to arrive on time or a little early at their destination, the issue of the intent of the law or the letter of the law often becomes a dilemma for drivers. Drivers overwhelmingly have decided that the intent of the law is paramount. When you consider the intent of the law, you have to consider and establish what your Expectations are of other people's actions and then adjust your actions accordingly. Therefore, drivers have established Expectations concerning other driver's conduct on the road.

One of the situations where Expectations have been created occurs at signal lights when they turn red. In one area of the country the Expectation had been established that when the light turns red, drivers will run the red light. This happens for known reasons, but the primary reason is that there is a delay before the cross traffic will enter the intersection! At many intersections after the light turns red there is a delay before the light turns green for the cross road traffic. Even without this added delay it takes a second or two of reaction time and a second or two to put an automobile into motion. These factors create a margin of safety for the driver to enter and cross the intersection after the light turns red because it will be a period of time, albeit short, before the cross traffic will be in the intersection. Therefore, when the traffic light turns yellow, drivers in one area (Rochester, New York) would actually not slow down if they believed they could make it through the light within the couple second safety factor delay. Since almost every driver shared this Expectation, drivers at cross roads in this area hesitate and double check to make sure the other drivers that would cross their path have actually stopped for the red light, or will stop. Their hesitation is based on a shared Expectation and drivers have adjusted their concept of Responsibility for themselves and others to insure that it is safe to proceed into the intersection.

In another area of the same state (New York City), drivers have established a different Expectation and established a totally different pattern at such intersections. When the light turns yellow those drivers stop. They will even slam on their breaks before the light turns red. Those drivers know the drivers on the cross road take off immediately when their light turns green. Some of the drivers at the cross roads will even 'jump the light', pulling out into the intersection while they still have a red light and the on-coming cross traffic still has a yellow light. In both communities the drivers have accepted their Responsibility and adapted to the Expectations of the other drivers.

For years, drivers have safely navigated past each other at intersections in these communities because they shared a common set of Expectations and Responsibility. [The Expectations established were derived from the Worldview of the majority of drivers in the community. Can you determine which Worldview created which Expectation? If you know the political makeup of the two municipal areas, then you only need one additional clue: The clue is to focus on the driver that is given the yellow and then the red lights and ask yourself how that driver views the driver in the cross traffic.] As you can see, the establishment of Expectations can create compatible situations for individuals in society. Drivers assumed Responsibility and made their own decisions because they knew the Expectations of other drivers in the area that they are in.

You can project for yourself what would happen if people who did not share the same Expectations met at an intersection – if drivers that 'jump the light' interacted with drivers that 'ran the light'. Obviously while the Responsibility of the driver would not change, because drivers would still make the decisions, the Expectations of the two groups are different and incompatible. The clash of Expectations would result in a shift in the safety characteristic of intersections. Such a clash of Expectations manifested itself in the Rochester, NY area. The safety characteristics of intersections shifted from safe to hazardous. That shift became a problem in need of a solution. The first solution imposed illuminated the Worldview structure of society that those in control of society desired to impose. Instead of driving patterns being controlled by modifying the Expectations and Responsibility of the driver by education or awareness programs, the Responsibility was transferred to the government. That political change in Direction resulted in government creating new features required to impose their Worldview solution. Those new features included new laws and traffic cameras. The characteristics of some elements already present in society shifted, such as the number of police and bureaucrats – they increased in number. Now that the solution is implemented, anyone and everyone going through a red light is given a ticket and fined. This solution forces a new Expectation, universally shared, onto the Drivers.

Society changed! The change was not the increase in police officers or the new laws or the new traffic cameras. The change was the imposition of a different Worldview structure and its solutions. Other features in society will now begin to shift their characteristics.

This Worldview solution may result in fewer accidents and injuries, and people in government may consider the increase in revenue to be a positive characteristic of the new traffic camera features. But, some people will consider the solution to have created undesirable features with negative characteristics and to be producing an undesirable shift in some unrelated features of society. Most people, oblivious to the changed Worldview, will just consider the positives and negatives to be a wash: If people did not pay the fine they would eventually be paying a repair bill, and perhaps a medical bill. No big deal! It doesn't matter that much.

But it does. No matter how you view the benefits of the traffic cameras and the shift to increased numbers of police patrols, the structure of society changed as society accommodated the needs of the Worldview solution that was being implemented.

Problems. The last point is a significant. Characteristics of features reflect society's response to the needs of the Worldview structure being pursued. A new structure for society will cause new features to be added and old features to be removed. The addition or deletion of features is easily and directly associated with the change in the Worldview. Once the relationship between the features and the Worldview is made, those features are largely ignored because it is obvious the Worldview of those in control of society would have to change to remove or reinstate the original features. It is the shifts in the characteristics of features that occur after the new Worldview is pursued that becomes the source of people's concerns. That concern can lead to new problems that need to be resolved. In the above example, the Worldview that created a structure for society where drivers responded to a need by establishing Expectations of other drivers is not the Worldview that created a structure for society where traffic cams were installed. The new traffic camera feature has created a need in society for drivers to adjust their Expectations. But, to what? Surely, drivers must now pay attention to the new traffic cams. If they do not pay attention they will pay a consequence. The traffic camera feature will cause a shift in a characteristic of driver's Expectations. The Expectations that guided driver's conduct at intersections for years will change. Whether new Expectations will be compatible with the Expectation of those who established

Mark E. Glogowski, Ph.D.

the new laws and traffic cameras is yet To Be Determined. But, because Responsibility has also changed relative to conduct at the intersection, and has not changed relative to the individual driving the automobile, it has yet To Be Determined how change in Expectation and Responsibility of drivers will play out. The Worldview change in Direction that resulted in government taking – and therefore enforcing – Responsibility may or may not be compatible with the Expectation and Responsibility of the drivers.

Summing up the relationships. It might seem strange to wait so long in the text to give these definitions and discuss these relationships between concepts, but if these definitions were given earlier, for the most part you would have just scratched your head and said to yourself, "What the heck is the author talking about?" Providing a definition for 'problems' in society for which solutions will be sought will illustrate this point. In the last example of 'running the red' versus 'jumping the light', the problem of safety was easily recognized by drivers. The feature in society – intersections – had a characteristic that was undesirable; it was not safe. People sought a solution so it would be safe to interact at intersections. Drivers recognized the problem, established an Expectation and that Expectation became the convention. Using this example as a starting point you can begin to see that problems are undesired shifts in the characteristics of features of society. Features themselves are not the problem. And, the creation of features or the loss of features is not a problem demanding a solution. Even the loss of a feature that had numerous positive and well known desirable characteristics that impacted everyone is not a problem. Undesirable characteristics of features are the problems. An undesirable shift in the characteristics of features caused by the loss of a desired feature or the creation of a feature is a problem. The problem requiring a solution is always the undesired shift in the characteristics of a feature of society. For example: the new traffic cameras are not a problem, but fines may cause economic stress, cameras may pick up activities that, while occurring on public land are still considered by the individuals to be private in nature. Errors in the mechanics of the camera, bureaucratic problems, and abuse may shift the Expectations of many people. Expectation is perhaps the most powerful and most easily forgotten concept in politics when change occurs. Expectations of those imposing solutions must be compatible with the Expectations of those that will be impacted by the solution. When Expectations are not compatible, society will clash. The most important fact to remember about Expectations is that individuals in society will strive to live up to the lowest Expectation established in society, because society will reinforce the lowest Expectation.

It is not the answer but the question that illuminates.

CHAPTER 31

IMMIGRATION – ILLEGAL IMMIGRATION

The Features, Characteristics, Structure, Issues, Problems, Solutions, Responsibility, Expectation, and Change in Immigration . . .

Immigration is an emotional issue where everyone's solutions tend to go to the extreme and people's bias tends to be intransigent. Whether you are in favor of the current immigration policy or opposed to it, everyone will agree that the current immigration policy of the United States is not working. This makes immigration an ideal issue to illustrate the relationships of concepts used that were reviewed in the previous chapter.

Why is the immigration policy not working? Hopefully, the following discussion will give you some political insight and understanding as to why the immigration issue remains unresolved.

If you personally know an immigrant, you tend to view other immigrants as decent people. If you do not know any immigrants, then immigrants are just suspicious people with strange customs and unknown backgrounds. Either way, immigrants are considered to be a catalyst for change in society. People fear change. Any change has the potential to cause people to not do, or to not enjoy, or to not anticipate or plan for, whatever it was that they used to do, they used to enjoy, and they used to anticipate and plan for. So yes, people even fear good change. When there are large numbers of immigrants, you can almost count on it – the changes will be dramatic and unwanted.

Immigrants are a catalyst, but solutions make change visible. Anyone that has observed the impact of immigrants on a community will confirm the fact that the presence of large numbers of immigrants can dramatically shift the characteristics of many features of society. Visible shifts make people concerned. Visible shifts in the characteristics of one feature of society that produce negative and undesirable impacts on characteristics of other features may scream for a solution. No one wants their society to visibly change. To prevent the visible change caused by immigrants, those in control of society in the past created a solution that was consistent with their Worldview's Direction and Approach. Their solution was a new immigration policy that would restrict who and how many people could immigrate. The policy was intended to prevent visible change. But their solution, based on their Direction and Approach, required new features to be created in society. The solution required new immigration laws, and new agencies, and established new Expectations. One observable result was a shift in the number of government agents (immigration, customs, and enforcement agents). A less noticed but almost as dramatic change was the loss of some features such as the groups and organizations that were helping immigrants get established in their new country. Those entities were no longer considered needed and were no longer utilized. The immigration problem today is that the immigration policy that was implemented did not solve the immigration problem. It merely created new problems and made the old problems worse, not better. Why?

Features versus Characteristics. Immigrants are an optional feature in society with their own unique characteristics, many of which can be quantified. Whether there are a lot of immigrants or a few immigrants in a society is a quantifiable characteristic of the feature 'immigrant'. Other quantifiable characteristics include such things as the average age of the immigrants, their education, and the number of children. But the feature 'immigrants' also have non-quantifiable characteristics, which includes such things as the fact that immigrants will work, they will take just about any job, and they will often work for minimal pay.

The characteristics of immigrants in and of themselves will not cause the structure of society to change no matter how dramatically the characteristics of immigrants' shift. The shift in the characteristics of immigrants just reflect the fact that immigrants will meet the needs of society as best they can. If society needs workers, immigrants will work. If society does not need workers, obviously immigrants will not be working. If society needs people to fill jobs and those jobs offer more pay, then immigrants will take the higher paying jobs (as would anyone that is qualified). If there are no higher paying jobs, immigrants will take the lower paying jobs. Immigrants also have a characteristic personality. Their personality will reflect a need or demand imposed by society. If society presents itself as hostile, immigrants will have no other choice but to reflect the hostility by protecting themselves as best they know how against the hostility. If immigrants effectively protect themselves, they will appear to display a characteristic of having a hostile personality. The point is, characteristics of features shift to reflect the response taken to meet the changing needs in society.

Whether the characteristics of features are viewed as being positive or negative depends entirely on the individual doing the viewing. From the perspective of long time residents in the community, the strange customs, strange foods, the foreign language, and the fact that immigrants tend to hang out with their own kind are all negative characteristics. An immigrant appearing to be unable to support themself is a negative characteristic. It is not only negative, it leads to the conclusion that immigrants have all the reasons they need to be motivated to become criminals. Since change is initiated by need, immigrants becoming criminals seems to be a very real possibility. It seems to be substantiated too, because all too often immigrants do become criminals; to the long time resident, one incident is defined as 'too often'. This characteristic of immigrants, appearing to be unable to support themselves, leads to the concern that immigrants have even more undesired and unwanted characteristics, and that immigrants create unwanted change in the community: They take jobs, demand services, burden local schools with their non-English speaking kids. If you get stoked up enough about immigrants, and you walk down the street and see an immigrant coming toward you, or worse, you see a group – a gang – of immigrants coming toward you . . . well, you just don't know what they intend to do. Immigrants are just plain scary.

Mark E. Glogowski, Ph.D.

Here is one Worldview solution: Just limit the number of immigrants that are allowed, make the rest illegal, and then get rid of them?

Legal and Illegal is a characteristic. An immigrant being legal or illegal is a characteristic of the immigrant feature of society. The characteristic does not create two separate features. Creating a characteristic of immigrants as illegal meets a need in society. The question is, what need? What created the need for some immigrants to be considered 'illegal'?

Hold off! Don't answer that question yet! If you try to answer the question you will be looking at other features of society and those features (employers, drug lords, gangs, welfare . . .) did not create the need that resulted in the presence of 'illegal' immigrants.

Needs are created by the structure imposed on society. The structure of society is determined by the Worldview of those placed in control of society. The need to label some immigrants as 'illegal' was created by the Worldview solution that was imposed on society. That Worldview solution considered immigrants, as a group, to be people that needed to be limited and controlled – Evil people. The solution that was implemented followed a structure for society that allowed the government to use the label 'illegal' and attach the label to some immigrants so they could be identified and deported. The new structure allowed the creation of a solution that required new immigration laws (features) and new agencies (the Immigration and Naturalization Service, Immigrations and Customs Enforcement) to be created. As these features were introduced to society, many other features began to change their characteristics. As the immigrants interacted with the 'laws of the land' the interaction caused the characteristics of immigrant to shift. The solution created the labels 'legal immigrant' and 'illegal immigrant': As these labels were applied, one of the needs of the new Worldview structure of society was met: Some immigrants are now called illegal. They can now be deported

Two Worldviews. Two Solutions. The fear of change led to the original solution to the immigration problem, which was to implement an immigration policy that would control the characteristic of the number of immigrants that were present.

The thought was, control the number of immigrants present, and where they came from, and you control change. Those in control of the United States government fashioned a solution using the Controller's Worldview (Conservative Republican) when they implemented the solution that created the feature of society referred to as an immigration policy. One of the immigration policy characteristics was a quota system, intended to control the number of immigrants.

The United States' immigration policy was unable to stop the flow of immigrants. All it did was define those that did not get prior approval and give them a label. "Illegal immigrants". The new feature of the 'immigration policy' not only shifted the characteristics of the immigrant feature of society, it split the immigrant feature into two seemingly separate features: Legal immigrants and illegal immigrants.

The continual flow of 'illegal immigrants' was shifting the characteristics of many features of society. There was a call for another solution. To prevent further changes in the features of society the Government changed the structure of society by changing the Approach, and adopted the Defender's (Liberal Democrat) Worldview solutions. This happened after the Defenders gained control of government. Government began to provide support to the immigrants: welfare, housing, medical care, education, driver's licenses, and what ever they seemed to need or desire. The new goal was to prevent the illegal immigrants from filling needs in society because when the 'illegal immigrants' fill the needs of society they become visible in society. Once visible, the 'illegal immigrants' were blamed for every shift observed in every characteristic of every feature. The Defender's new immigration policy solution was intended to prevent immigrants from changing the characteristics of other features in society by making sure they had no reason to fill those needs. The government began to cater to all of the needs of 'illegal immigrants'.

The U.S. immigration policy creates unwanted change.
The structure of society in the United States was changed by the Controller's and Defender's as they implemented their Worldview solutions. The clash between features that existed, and that still

exist in society, and the many laws, rules and regulations created by the immigration policy, have produced incompatible Expectations amongst the government, the immigrants, and the residents caught in the middle. The immigration policy implemented has turned out to be an abysmal solution. Here are some of the features of society in the U. S. whose unwanted characteristics can be traced in full or in part to the United States immigration policy:

> Employers are considered Evil and criminal when they employ illegal immigrants and make them productive members of society.

> The welfare, health, and educational systems of the states attempting to prevent illegal immigrants from filling needs in society are overburdened.

> Hardships caused by the increased welfare expenses has placed an economic burden on everyone (because of the benefits given to immigrants), which subsequently impacts many other features of society.

> A tsunami of drugs is pouring into the country, because illegal commerce is a viable means of support available to illegal immigrants.

> Gang wars related to drug trafficking is occurring on both sides of the Mexican border and has resulted in so many murders that the number of murders along the border has been reported to be of the same order of magnitude as the number of people killed in the entire country of Iraq where formalized hostilities raged. A slaughter is going on along the border – and illegal immigrants are blamed[26].

With all the negatives people associate with immigrants, it is not difficult to understand why people have come to the conclusion that the immigration problem is out of control and that we have a situation in society that just should not be. How much more out of control will it get? The number of people arriving by means other than through the official process is enormous. Those people are the illegal immigrants! If the same Worldviews that were used to create the 'illegal immigrant' problem are used to create the solutions to these shifts in the characteristics of society's features that have become the current problem, the solutions will only shift the characteristics of features in society to a further extreme from what is already present in society. An example of such a solution is the Alabama immigration policy, just signed into law[27]. It not only views 'illegal immigrants' as Evil, but the law considers Evil anyone that might help an 'illegal immigrant'. Anyone! Anyone, that is, except official government agencies. Government agencies can continue to service these individuals, providing food, housing, driver's licenses, even cash (welfare) – all in compliance with the structure their Worldview has created for society. In that Worldview structure government attends to the welfare of the individual 'illegal immigrant' with the goal of preventing the 'illegal immigrants' from changing the other features of society. The Alabama law is nothing more than a continuation of a failed policy that will cause society to become even more, "something that just should not be."

How much more can governments do? Many of our governments have already bled their financial coffers dry just trying to cope with the current demands that immigrants – both legal and illegal – make for services. How far can this solution be pushed? If the Defenders (Liberal Democrat) pursue a search for a larger, more effective solution with more government involvement and control over society, or if the Controllers (Conservative Republican) implement a solution that labels even more people as Evil and cast their net of regulations and controls over an even broader spectrum of society – either way – it will just be just a lot more of the same failed solutions. The features of our society that seem out of control were shaped that way to meet the needs of the structure imposed on society by the current solution that was implemented: The current immigration policy. Continuing those policies under a more stringent form can only result in an even more dramatic shift in the characteristics of the features of society. Your freedoms and Good Will are a couple features that will display the largest undesirable shift.

Not how the world should work. The implementation of an immigration policy was intended to be a solution that would stabilize the characteristics of features of society from the impact of hoards of individuals – millions of individuals – crossing our borders. The current United States' immigration policy did not work. It does not work. It can not work! When people make the decision to emigrate from their homeland they have already determined for themself that a new place to call home is worth any pain they would have to endure: They want a better life! Being captured and sent back to their homeland is not considered a hardship; it is just a detour. The threat of death in the back of a truck in the Arizona desert, being shot by a drug lord, being shot and killed by border guards – these are all acceptable risks. Ask yourself, when people want to emigrate out of their country and immigrate into another, should they be subjected to dangers, hardships, even death because of the deliberate hostile actions of any government? We did not think so in Berlin! Why do we think it is OK to have such a policy here in America – or anywhere for that matter?

People want a better life. The current U.S. immigration policy causes people to die just because they are pursuing a better life. If this fact bothers you, and this is an unacceptable characteristic of our society, then think about a new Direction and Approach. For a minute, set aside your emotions and the demands you make of government – which were probably instilled by PU statements – and consider the following:

Most of the immigrants, legal and illegal, just want a better life for themselves and their families, and they desire to be productive members of society.

If you were in their position, how would you want yourself and your family to be treated?

A conundrum (a puzzle, a riddle, a contradictory situation) . . Take a closer look at the concept of 'Direction'. Direction is the first of the two elements that create your Worldview. If we are going to create a new solution, the first thing we need to do is to determine a Direction. You are probably saying to yourself right now something like,

"Well! The Direction has to be 'Government'. Doesn't it? After all, Direction refers to who is making the decisions. How can the individual, the immigrant, be given the authority to make the decision? They do not even live in the country yet. It is the government's responsibility to serve and protect its citizens. How can the government perform its duties and live up to its responsibilities if immigrants are allowed to make their own decisions concerning their immigration to another country?"

And you might even be thinking that it doesn't matter whether you believe the individual should be Responsible for themself. When it comes to immigration, there has to be government involvement. It can't be any other way. Can it? Perhaps there can only be one answer to the first Political Interrogatory when you are looking for a Direction to take when coming up with solutions to the immigration problem. After all, if government is to live up to its responsibilities to its citizens, then the 'Direction' will have to default to the government making the decisions. It does, doesn't it?

And now we are back again to, how can you have individuals making decisions for themself concerning immigrating into any country when the government is responsible for the security and protection of its citizens? The immigrants and government are going to clash if they both think they have the right to make that decision. The first Political Interrogatory has created a conundrum when it comes to immigration. Whose decisions dominate?

Clarifying the Conundrum. Let's make the conflict in the conundrum a bit clearer before we tackle it. The first Political Interrogatory appears to be inappropriate because it seems to apply to two related but different decisions under two different circumstances made at two different points in time. The first is the immigrant making the decision to emigrate. The second is the decision regarding whether the immigrant can stay.

Lets accept the following statement, for now, as a premise upon which to work, and then look at the immigrant problem again: Government has the responsibility to protect its citizens against unwanted change. If the individual desires to emigrate from their country to another country and the government in the other country says no – isn't the government and the immigrant going to clash? Everyone knows unwanted changes will occur if hoards of unwanted immigrants are allowed to enter the country – exactly the type of change everyone claims the government is responsible to prevent. One can only conclude that the government must have the final authority to make the decisions concerning foreigners coming into, and remaining in, their country. How can an immigrant that is not a citizen of a country make the decision concerning their coming into a country and staying without overriding the responsibility of the government? How can the first Political Interrogatory apply to the issue of immigration? The only Direction that seems possible is Government. If you answer the first Political Interrogatory, as it applies to the issue of immigration, with "the individual is responsible for themself" you create the conundrum!

Resolving the Conundrum. Government was created to protect its citizens. That is a given. Government will necessarily be involved in the implementation of any solution to the immigration problem. That, too, is a given. However, the fact that the government has a role in the immigration process does not preclude the Direction as determined by the first Political Interrogatory. Who should be responsible for the welfare of the individual, even when the individual is an immigrant, has little to do with whether or not there is a role for government.

The Role of Government. The choice of Direction, as determined by the first Political Interrogatory, defines the role of government just as it defines the role of the individual! What is intended by the need to choose a 'Direction', as determined by the first Political Interrogatory, is that when you create a solution, does the solution go in the Direction of giving the government the authority to make all the decisions concerning how the immigrant will be cared for? Or, is there an Expectation that the role of government is to empower the immigrant and to create the Expectation that the immigrant will take care of their own needs? If the latter is the case, then the role of government will be to empower the individual immigrant with the authority to make their own decisions and to pursue their own goals concerning their own personal welfare. The Worldview of those in charge of society can create a structure and role for government that helps empower the immigrant to achieve their ultimate goal- which is to live a better life.

An Imaginary Line. The borders of a country are not real. They are imaginary lines created in space that help a society determine where the structure of one society stops and the structure of another starts. Physical features on earth only help identify where those imaginary lines are located. When an individual walks across an imaginary line something changes. That something is 'Expectations'. It has always been an Expectation of every society that when an individual crosses the imaginary lines called borders, that the individual will comply with and be subject to the laws of the society on that side of the border. When an individual crosses a border, the requirement to comply with the laws of the land is the only change that occurs. Placing of quotas, language requirements, monetary requirements, ethnic, cultural, or any other requirement on the characteristics of the traveler will not eliminate the requirement for the individual, the traveler, crossing the imaginary line, to conform to the laws of the land as set up by those in charge of society. Putting up a physical barrier does not negate this Expectation. Walls and border guards are intended to restrict and stop individuals trying to cross the imaginary line. They are not intended to change any Expectation of any individual crossing a border. Again, this situation relates to the conundrum and the establishment of clashing Expectations. The individual is not bound to the laws on the other side of the imaginary line until they cross the line. When the individual makes the decision to emigrate and cross the imaginary line, they have the right to cross the imaginary line. But, if that imaginary line is the U.S. border, they instantly lose that right just because they did cross the line that they had the right to cross before they crossed it. See the problem? A conundrum of Expectations!

Expectations from needs of conflicting Worldviews. Government is a feature of society. It can be re-structured, grown in power, shrunk in power, divided, combined, and manipulated in any fashion desired by its citizens. No matter how it changes, the government will remain a feature of society serving a function. Immigrants, too, are a feature of most societies. Immigrants have certain needs. The Expectation of both of these features is that their needs will be met and that a natural shift in the characteristics of other features in society will occur to accommodate the needs of government and of the immigrants. The features of government and immigrants have to interrelate, they have to be compatible, and they have to be complementary in order for society to function smoothly. Whether these two features are compatible depends upon the structure of society as determined by the Direction and Approach of those involved. For the government, the Direction and Approach are determined by the structure of society created by the Worldview of those placed in control of government. For the immigrant, the Direction and Approach is that of the Worldview held by the immigrant themself. The Direction and Approach for both must be compatible. If the features of government and immigrants develop incompatible needs and require conflicting shifts in the characteristics of other features in society, the two will develop incompatible Expectations. They will clash. Violently!

A clash between groups that hold different Expectations is a common occurrence in society. We saw it when we discussed the Expectations established by drivers. As long as the drivers only interacted with a group of people that shared the same Expectation there was no problem. But when individuals did not share common Expectations, there was a clash – or rather crash. The clashes caused by the development of incompatible societal Expectations between immigrants and government will also result in chaos and the creation of an irresolvable political Gap for both groups.

It has always been a belief in American society that free men of Good Will should be allowed to freely cross these imaginary lines as long as they are 'men of Good Will' and they obey the laws and customs of the society they are visiting. It had been a standard in the United States that all men are created equal. It is also a standard that all men are basically 'Good'; innocent until proven otherwise. The unstated conclusion, which the country was founded on, was that all Good men are welcome. Immigrants

The Political Primer

desiring a better life can not consider themself anything other than 'Good'. If they considered themself to be 'Evil' then why would they be seeking a better life? Just stands to reason. The Expectation of the immigrant would be that Good men of Good Will are welcome anywhere.

So what happens when these 'Good men of Good Will' are confronted with a society whose government is pursuing a Worldview that views all men as Evil? Obviously there will be a conflict of Expectations. When the needs of these two features establish and demand different Expectations of society, Reality will become for both groups a situation 'that just should not be'.

Consider your Worldview. In order for your Reality to become consistent with your Worldview concerning immigration, the Expectations for both the government and the immigrant will have to be consistent with the Expectation established by your Worldview. This can only happen when the features of society reflect the Worldview Direction and Approach to solutions derived from the Worldview you embraced. If government and the immigrant follow a Worldview that is not your Worldview, your political Gap will continue to grow. All three features of society (you, government, and the immigrant) need to share the same Expectations.

CHAPTER 32

FINAL COMMENT

You should by now have a pretty clear idea which Worldview you embrace, and hopefully you have a little better understanding of the interrelationships of society's structure, features, and characteristics, and how Expectations play a role in society. You should also be able to find solutions using your Worldview where you say to yourself, "Now that is how society should work. That is the right solution!" You should also be able to create three other distinctly different solutions using the other three Worldviews where you tell yourself, "Now that is not how the world should work. Those are real, but wrong solutions!"

The reality of life is that there are solutions you accepted as being appropriate, even though you knew they would never come close to creating a society you wanted to live in. In these cases, instead of pursuing a Worldview solution that changed Reality, you accepted a Worldview solution that accommodated reality. The solution at the time may have seemed appropriate because it met the needs of Reality as you saw it. But, the solution you accepted was created by someone pursuing another Worldview. You accepted the solution, even though it would not produce a world you want to live in because 'that's the way things are'. 'Someone has to do something'. If these, or any similar excuses, are the reason you support a solution to any issue, you have been PUed! If you cling to any solution that is not 100% consistent with your Worldview you have been PUed. You were led to believe that your Worldview is something too idealistic to be implemented at the present time. One way to determine if you have been PUed is to ask yourself if you become emotional when the subject is brought up. If you do, then you probably have been PUed. The immigration issue is not an exception to this phenomenon. If you become emotional talking about the immigration issue, if you adamantly, perhaps even angrily, cling to your solution because you can't trust immigrants, immigrants are criminals because they broke our immigration laws, immigrants are taking jobs from hard working Americans, immigrants are druggies, immigrants are members of gangs – any non-Worldview justification you can come up with – you have been PUed. PU statements have nothing to do with Direction and Approach. They may have a Direction or they may have an Approach, but the fact is, PU statements are intended to prevent you from considering your preferred Direction and Approach to society's structure. PU statements are intended to keep you from reflecting on your Worldview standard of how the world should work.

Don't be duped!

If you start with your Worldview and then create a solution that is consistent with your Worldview, you will find society will soon create compatible Expectations for and between every feature.

Beware of the PU statements Did you figure out what the PU statement was that influenced your desire for government to solve the immigration problem? The PU statement, to be effective must immediately cause you to suppress your Worldview. Without your Worldview there is no other side of the political Gap! See if this happens when you read the PU statement below. Consider the fact that the only act of the immigrant was crossing an imaginary line and that the Expectation has always been that all 'men of Good Will' are welcome as long as they obey the laws of the society of the country on the other side of the border once they get there.

PU Statement: Illegal immigrants are illegal because they came into the country illegally, in violation of the U.S. immigration policy.

You can not have free men of Good Will traveling freely if PU statements such as these are allowed to influence the laws of society!

EPILOG

WHAT IS MIGHTIER THAN THE PEN

To be politically wise you must know your Worldview and pursue your Worldview.

When you say to yourself, 'That just should not be!', 'That is just wrong!', 'That is not how our society should work', you are acknowledging that a political Gap exists between your Reality, which is how you perceive society is working, and your Worldview, which is how you believe society should work. As your Reality and your Worldview diverge, the political Gap widens. As your political Gap widens you will become increasingly agitated and motivated to do something about the Reality you are experiencing. When your Gap increases to a point where your Reality is no longer acceptable you will do something. You will get involved. The problem is, get involved doing what? How do you make Reality become what it should be? Sure, you can pick up a copy of <u>Politics for Dummies</u> or some similar publication and follow the suggestions published, but without a clear understanding of your own Worldview, all you will do – all you can do – is agitate and create chaos in the hopes that someone, somewhere, will take notice of you pathetically agitating in a political fog. If you desire to make a difference and you allow yourself to become emotionally driven to change Reality, you will be a Pawn ripe for the picking. You will become the political Pawn of the first politician that throws a PU statement at you.

Politics is not complicated . . . Politics actually boils down to two facts:

1. There are only four Worldviews.
2. Politics is about making your Worldview society's Reality.

Mark E. Glogowski, Ph.D.

The only Worldview that impacts society is the shared Worldview of the group of individuals that have been placed in positions of authority over society. Currently, our political process lets you participate in the selection of those individuals. Their Worldview's Direction and Approach will determine the solutions that will be implemented. Those solutions will determine the features of society. As features of society are created and other are eliminated, the characteristics of the remaining features of society will readjust to reflect the Worldview of those in authority, and society will or will not be what it should be.

You do not have to wait until unwanted features of society appear and characteristics of features undesirably shift. You can determine whether the society being created is a society you want to live in by simply reflecting on your Worldview and then ask, "Is the Worldview of those individuals given authority over society the same Worldview you hold?". If your Worldview is not the same as theirs, you will not like the society they are creating. Your political Gap will increase!

The reason politics is all about you is due to the fact that you have the power to create the world you want to live in. When the Reality you experience is not consistent with your Worldview you will be motivated to do something. That something is called 'politics'. But to be effective in politics you must take three steps before you act. If you take them you will become politically astute and effective, and no one will ever be able to use you as a political Pawn.

> First step: Determine your Worldview.
> Second step: Determine the candidates' Worldview.
> Third step:
>   a) Decide to support the candidates who are pursuing your Worldview, or
>   b) Decide to become a candidate and solicit the support of others who hold your Worldview.

Take these three steps before you act and you will be politically wise.

Getting you motivated. Every candidate that wants to get elected needs to motivate you to get involved. They need you to give them your support even if that support is nothing more than to just stand up, vote, and be counted. The easiest way to get you to become involved in politics is to have you begin to believe that your Reality

The Political Primer

is not right. Politicians know that if they can widen your political Gap you will become agitated enough to get involved in politics. This is why politics is all about you. You need to be motivated before you will get involved, and candidates need you to be involved.

Candidates search for issues that you are interested in. Then they focus on whatever aspect of those issues you are most passionate about. Once the candidates have determined your interests and your passions, they set about to widen your Gap. They need you to believe that Reality is not right – that reality needs to change. The goal of every candidate on the campaign trail is to widen your political gap sufficiently to get you to become upset enough to rally in the streets, demonstrate, protest, and if necessary, become a candidate yourself!

Candidates look for PU statements that are effective, and issues that you are emotional about. Then they throw those issues and PU statements at you relentlessly. They know that, under the right conditions there is no limit to how wide your political Gap can appear to be.

You are motivated. Now what? Once you have been motivated, you have a choice of two political activity paths. You can either become a political Pawn or you can become a politically astute citizen. The choice is yours. Make it consciously!

You were given a free will so that you can make decisions.

To become a political Pawn all you need to do is to accept as political wisdom one or more of the PU statements thrown at you. If you do you will suppress your Worldview. You are now a political Pawn. The only benefit to becoming a political Pawn is that you will become emotionally satisfied. As a Pawn in the political process you will not only be emotional, you will become intensely emotional, and you will become intensely politically active. Your anger will have you demonstrating in the streets. You may even be willing to get arrested. After all – Somebody has to do something!

As a Pawn, your PU statement induced Reality will be grossly distorted. There will not only be a Gap between your distorted Reality and your Worldview, the distance between your Reality as you are now perceiving it and your Worldview will be a gigantic chasm – because your Worldview is nowhere in sight.

Mark E. Glogowski, Ph.D.

There is no 'other side' of the political Gap. But that won't matter to you because the candidates that strove to get you to abandon your Worldview want you to put your entire trust in their hands. They have a solution! Your candidate has the solution! It will not matter to you that the candidate is advocating a solution derived from a Worldview that you actually disagree with. To you, that won't matter because the candidate is 'the best qualified' – or the candidate possesses some other PU initiated mis-belief quality.

To be a political Pawn you must suppress your Worldview. To remain a pawn you must believe your Worldview is irrelevant!

The alternative political course of action requires you to understand your Worldview and to seek out those candidates that will actually pursue your Worldview. Unfortunately, the candidates that adhere to your Worldview may not be as charismatic, or may not have the most experience, or they may lack public speaking skills, or they may have irritated you on some topic, or . . . The list of reasons why you might not support a candidate is endless. And, if you are like most voters, even if there are a thousand reasons to support a candidate, one negative will trump all of the positives and the candidate will lose your vote. For the astute political voter, the Statesmen and the Politicians, there is one reason to support a candidate that will trump a thousand negatives. The one reason that you should <u>always</u> use to justify supporting a candidate, a reason that will trump a thousand negatives is this:

The candidate shares your Worldview of how the world should work!

The political path you take is not a decision the politician can make. The political path you take is up to you. You can either grab on to a PU statement and then go with the flow because it is emotionally appealing, or you can spend the time and make the effort to determine how you want the world to work – which takes nothing more than answering the two Political Interrogatories that define the Worldviews. Ponder over how Worldviews impact society and then commit yourself to deliberately pursuing that Worldview.

Remember: *The goal of politics is to make society work the way you believe society should work.*

Worldviews and History. Now that you have finished the Political Primer, you will not be able to review any history of mankind without realizing that throughout history three Worldviews have been dominant: The **Enforcer's**, the **Defender's**, and the **Controller's**.

History is filled with rulers and conquerors who held one of these three Worldviews. They have, in one form or another, imposed their Worldview structure on the citizens of their country. If the citizens resisted, there was no hesitation to use force. If protests escalated to rebellion, rulers had no hesitancy to escalate the conflict to civil war. The use of force is always an option to rulers that hold these Worldviews. More often than not, when the rulers of one country considered the structure of society of another country to be unacceptable, especially when that country was a neighbor, rulers would invade. For these individuals force, even war, is an acceptable method to impose a Worldview. After all, war is just an alternative to 'politics'.

History is outlined, punctuated, and differentiated by the use of force: Wars, uprisings, rebellions, civil wars, and all kinds of internal strife. We study these events because each event has led to changes in the features of society; some dramatic, rapid, and visible to all, and some not so dramatic. We study the causes of war and look at the features that existed in society during times of peace and during times of war. Features change. New features appeared. Each time existing features changed, the change was observed to occur to accommodate new features that appeared in society. What is not emphasized in most historical text is the fact that the real change that occurred in society was a change in the Worldview being implemented by the individual(s) who gained control of society – the leaders. Everything else immediately or eventually just reflected that change.

Three Features of Society. There are three features of society that have been present throughout history regardless of which one of the three Worldviews was being pursued.

First feature of society: there was always a <u>ruling class</u>. Each of the three dominant Worldviews creates a ruling class! While some of the rulers had the best interests of their citizens at heart, others had been absolutely ruthless in their dominion over society.

Mark E. Glogowski, Ph.D.

Exercising their power and control over society for their personal gain and glory, the ruling class required two other features to exist in society – restrictive laws, and a means to enforce them.

The ruling class invariably created solutions for problems where the solution was just to pass a law. Their <u>restrictive laws</u> were the solution. If the restrictions placed on the citizens of the country became too oppressive and citizens objected, ruling classes hava never hesitated to implement their restrictive laws as a feature of society using force. Force is a feature present in all three Worldview societies. The citizen either conformed to the law of the land or they lost their freedom. Death, the result of the extreme use of force was always, and still is, an option for those that truly do not want to accept the Reality of the structure of society that was created by the ruling class's Worldview

The rule of law, even today, is imposed at the edge of a sword and the point of a gun. The rulers pursuing these three Worldviews are quite comfortable imposing their Worldview using force. The point of a gun is very effective at producing compliant and obedient citizens and neighbors: When you are looking at the point of a gun, the only other option to obedience is usually unacceptable.

<u>Force</u> is a feature of society with extremes in its characteristics. Force can shift from intolerable suffering and total obliteration to the other extreme of negative force, i.e., appeasement and pacification. The fact that history is punctuated by episodes where force is used during times of strife is a logical Expectation derived from the structure of societies created by these three Worldviews.

Only one Worldview's structure of society minimizes force to the point that it is not an element of any significance in any solution. Only one Worldview refuses to implement solutions where the method of implementation is force. That Worldview is the Advocate's Worldview. The Advocate's Worldview can not be imposed by force because the Advocate's Worldview is only functional when society is comprised of men of Good Will and people who at all times conduct themselves with respect for others. Respect is not a characteristic that can be imposed at the point of a gun. In a society structured by the Advocate's Worldview there is no Governing versus Governed class system, so no one individual or group has the right to force another individual or group to do something they don't want to do. The Expectation established by the Advocate's Worldview is that everyone will take care of themselves, help other people in need, and respect the rights of others at all times. When a wrong occurs, the Expectation is that the person that committed the wrong will right the wrong, even at their own personal expense and to their personal detriment. The Advocate's Worldview sets very high the lowest Expectation for the conduct of man. In spite of the high Expectation standards, there are those individuals that hold to a different Worldview. Those individuals must be dealt with. Thereby, there is a role for government, and that role is to interact with citizens, and with other countries, when disagreements and disruptions occur between individuals and groups, domestic and international, that can not be resolved by the individuals and groups.

What is least understood about the Advocate's Worldview is that an Advocate does believe in the use of deadly force by an individual against another individual. This position seems almost contradictory to the Expectation that people are Good and that people respect the rights and property of others. How can Good people use deadly force and still consider themself to be Good people?

The use of force is not limited to a matter of survival of the individual. For an Advocate, deadly force is acceptable when an individual harms another or steals or destroys their property. There is no greater wrong in the Advocate's Worldview than not defending yourself, your family, your neighbors, your acquaintances, and even strangers against harm. Just as seriously is the wrong of not protecting the property that belongs to you or to others. When the harm or the loss can be prevented with deadly force, in the Advocate's Worldview structure, deadly force is justified. The perpetrator of an assault upon another and the perpetrator of theft of another's property is committing the single greatest crime against the Advocate's society that is possible – the individual is failing to respect the rights of others. By failing to respect the lives and property of others the perpetrator is not living up to the lowest Expectation set by the Advocate's Worldview. If society, which in the Advocate's Worldview is the individual, fails to enforce the lowest Expectation, that Expectation will cease to be the lowest Expectation. A lower Expectation will be created by society's failure to respond forcefully to keep the Expectation high. If the obligation to respect other people and their property is lowered, the Advocate's Worldview structure will begin to disappear and Reality of society will begin to become something that 'just should not be'. If those in control of society do not create and implement a solution that empowers the individual to address and solve the problem, the continued erosion of the Expectations will result in a group of people looking for any other solution – any non-Advocate Worldview solution.

The Advocate's Worldview structure extends the obligation to defend the lives, wellbeing and property of others to all levels of government. At the federal level, government has the responsibility to defend its citizens against any foreign attack and protect its citizens from any harm caused by any source outside the country. Government would be expected to be well prepared militarily. Government is also obligated, because of the Expectation created by the Advocate's Worldview, to respect the rights of neighboring countries and refrain from using force in any offensive manner[28]. With modern means of travel, every country in the world today is effectively a neighboring country.

The Advocate's Worldview: Freedom and Equality. In the Enforcer's, Defender's, and Controller's Worldview societies there is no true freedom for the populous. Rulers of societies following two of these Worldviews, the Enforcer and Controller, have an Expectation that people are Evil. Government must set limits and restraints on the Evil people. The Defender's Worldview does not consider people Evil, but considers it government's responsibility to tend to the needs of its citizens. Therefore, the rulers pursuing one of these Worldviews will quickly resort to force in order to impose their rule of law, demand obedience from its citizens, and to keep order in society.

Only the Advocate's Worldview will actually result in freedom and equality for all.

Can this be true? If you want freedom and equality, where there is no ruling class, can it be true that only one Worldview will provide that reality? Because if it is true and you want freedom and equality for all, then only one Worldview can be the 'right'

The Political Primer

Worldview! This is not what was implied in Chapter 5 when it was stated that any answer to the Political Interrogatories is the right answer and that any Worldview you hold is the right Worldview. If this were true, that only one Worldview will produce a Reality with equality and freedom for all, wouldn't someone of importance have pointed this out before now?

Well someone did!

The Christian Reality. The Advocate's Worldview did not become a reality until long after the concept was first championed – over 2,000 years ago. Jesus Christ advocated that you are basically Good – that is why Christians believe Jesus came to save us. He also taught that you, and only you, are Responsible for yourself. He advocated that you should be making all the decisions on issues that impact you. He taught that you should respect the decisions of other people, and their property. He taught that you should be able to make any agreement you desire with another person as long as that agreement does not adversely impact a third person. He advocated that those in charge of society should never give themselves a benefit that is not equally shared by all those that are governed. He advocated that you help your family, friends, neighbors, and even strangers. He even taught that government should never confiscate the proceeds of your labor as a tax.

By promoting his Advocate Worldview, Jesus caused quite a stir in his lifetime. He advocated a structure for society that had never existed. He taught against the structure of all the societies that existed from the time of Moses until and including when he was alive. From a secular perspective, Jesus Christ was crucified because he was changing people's minds about how society should be structured. The rulers of his time did not appreciate his political rabble rousing activities. From a secular viewpoint, Jesus was crucified because he wanted to emphasize that how we live is worth dying for. "How we live is worth dying for" is a theme heard often in history. The theme is not a foreign concept to religions or politics.

It is Common Sense. Every Christian, every politician, every American voter, and anyone that is truly interested in politics in their country, no matter which country they live in, should read two books. The first book is The Political Teachings of Jesus, by Tod Lindburgh[29].

Mark E. Glogowski, Ph.D.

This book discusses what Jesus Christ taught about how you and I should get along here on earth. Lindburgh strips away the miraculous, the theological, and the religious, and then discusses the political concepts that Jesus taught concerning those that govern, about the law, about the role you should play, and your duty and obligations to society. Once you have read Lindburg's book, read Thomas Payne's essays collectively titled Common Sense. If you can not find a reproduction of Thomas Pane's essays, you can find the essays reproduced in the second half of Glenn Beck's book titled Common Sense30. After you have read these two documents you will be able to come to no other conclusion than that the United States was founded on political principles taught by Jesus Christ. At the time the country was founded it was not known whether any country founded on those principles could survive. No country on earth was ever structured around the Worldview that people are Responsible for themself and that people are basically Good. Never in history had this been attempted: People empowered to govern and rule and take care of themselves!!? And would willingly help others!!? A society based on the Advocate's Worldview. It was an American Experiment, indeed!

The Constitution of the United States. It has never been done. A nation built on the Advocate's Worldview? Would it work? Could it survive? There were some people who wanted to pursue a structure for the United States that would create a society reflecting one of the other three Worldviews. The Worldview used by the founding fathers of the United States to draft the Constitution is revealed in the writings of people like Thomas Paine. The Worldview was that of the Advocate; a strong belief in individual rights that include the freedom to make your own decisions, individual Responsibility, and a limited, non-intrusive role for government in society. The original concept of a limited government referred to a limited role for government; it referred to government being restricted so that it was not able to intrude on the lives of its citizens. The US government today does not seem to be limited and it intrudes on every aspect of American life.

The American Experiment. Jesus Christ taught that society should be re-structured so that people would respected individual freedom and individual Responsibility. He advocated that all decisions be made at the smallest organization level possible – and that level was the individual if the individual was the only person to be impacted. Jesus advocated a society that consisted of men of Good Will, exercising their God given Free Will to make their own decisions, responsible for their own welfare, respectful of the rights of others, with a government that did not intrude on their lives and did not confiscate their earnings. Where two or more are gathered together, there is where he insisted the Advocate's Worldview reign supreme. The United States Constitution was created following these principles – the political principles taught by Jesus. What made the United States unique in the history of the world, and what makes us unique today, was the Worldview that was followed to create the structure for the fledgling country. Following that Worldview Direction and Approach to the development of society resulted in the drafting of the Constitution of the United States.

We are not a 'Christian' nation because we do not require people to be Christians to be part of our society – and we do not force them to become Christians. However, we are a nation founded on the principle of respect for all men regardless of what they believe – as Jesus taught.

America was founded on the political teachings of Jesus Christ.

It worked! The American Experiment was a tremendous success. Following the Worldview of the Advocate, America became the land flowing in milk and honey. People around the world began to dream about coming to America.

Unfortunately, Americans became comfortable with the fact that the structure of society, an Advocate's society, was fixed in the Constitution and that the Reality of life in the United States was becoming consistent with the Advocate Worldview. As the Reality of life became more and more consistent with the Advocate's Worldview, a Worldview enjoyed and pursued by the majority of the people in America, Americans began to step away from politics. Life was good. The majority of Americans became silent, detached from politics. Their political Gap had disappeared.

A turn for the worst. Well, life was good for the Advocates. It wasn't so good for those individuals that desired to pursue one of the other three Worldviews. They became upset. Their

Mark E. Glogowski, Ph.D.

reality was becomming something that just should not be. To them, government should not be sitting on the sidelines while people suffered. Government had to start doing something. In the Worldview of the non-Advocate, people were making bad, stupid decisions. Government had to do something, even if it was only to step in and begin restricting the actions of people. For the non-Advocate, the political Gap was enormous and getting greater. As a result, those individuals adhering to the Enforcer's, Defender's, and Controller's Worldviews became politically active. They gained control over society and began implementing their solutions. Their changes to the structure of the American society caused many new features to appear in American life, slowly at first. As new laws were created, those laws reflected the non-Advocate Worldviews of the people they put in control. Change in the United State began to become visible. Change increased at an ever faster pace as government imposed its will on the people with every new law and regulation. As the numbers of non-Advocates elected to office increased, one issue at a time the Advocate's Worldview structure for the United States began to disappear.

The structure of society in the United States today has very little resemblance to the structure of a society that believes people are responsible for themself and that people are basically Good. The government of the United States today can not be characterized as being 'non-intrusive' on the lives of its citizens. The government has taken on the role of decision maker and has assumed total Responsibility for the health, safety, and welfare of the individual. The Expectation of the conduct of individuals in society has been lowered and laws have become harsher and more restrictive as a result. People no longer pursue the Advocate's Worldview Direction and Approach for any solution to any problem. Instead people demand that government focus on controlling the Reality of mankind's Evil side. The Expectations of society have become so low that any Advocate based solution today is ridiculed as being close to lunacy. The Advocate's Worldview is dependent upon a high Expectation of respect for the rights, life, and property of others. Society has no Expectation that anyone will respect the rights, property, or life of another if they can justify a wrong. Those in control willingly pursue the people's demands to control

The Political Primer

the Evil in society; doing so is consistent with their Worldview. In the minds of those individuals in authority over society, Evil people in society can and will be controlled by government's stepped up efforts to enforce the Laws of the Land! Everyone's conduct will be restricted by new laws, even those hypocritical enough to consider themself to be honest, Good people.

As the structure of society increasingly reflected the Defender's and Controller's Worldview, local governments began to adopt the Enforcer's attitude that society has problems and that it is the local government's ultimate Responsibility to implement solutions to those problems whether you, the citizen, like them or not. In many cases you don't even have to consider a situation to be a problem. Government will impose their rules and codes on you for any reason they desire . . . because they can . . . it is their law.

Society's features change in response to changes in society's structure.

Synergism between Issues, Problems, Features, and Characteristics. There is a synergistic force in the relationship between the various features of society. When features are compatible they have a calming effect on society. When features are incompatible they generate a mutually shared irritation that grows until both features have developed characteristics 'that just should not be'. When this happens, the features become the issue and the shift in characteristic of the features becomes the problem. Preventing the shift from occurring or returning the characteristic to its former state becomes the goal of a solution. Every solution will cause some combination of new features appearing in society, some features disappearing and others shifting in their characteristics.

A new feature that causes no shift in any other feature of society is not a problem. But, creating a new feature that causes no shift in the characteristics of any other feature in society is also not a solution: It caused no shift in the characteristics of any other feature! An old feature that disappeared may be missed, but it is not a problem. What is a problem is the shift in characteristics of features in society that remain when an old feature disappears.

When the United States Congress began to pursue a non-Advocate Worldview, the structure of the U.S. society began to change. There was a cascade effect. The new laws created to support the non-Advocate Worldview solutions caused the characteristics of many features of society to shift. Those shifts in characteristics were viewed as problems that required additional solutions, which resulted in more new laws and other new features to appear. These new features caused more shifts, and more laws, and more shifts . . . a cascade effect. The cascade is synergistic because every interaction between features of society either relieved the irritation or caused additional irritation and shifts in characteristics. Each solution implemented that supported the non-Advocate Worldview's structure for society slowly caused the United States to reflect the Controllers and Defender's Worldview. The mad cycle of shifts, problems, solutions, new features, shifts, problems, solutions, new features, . . . continues, and will continue until the entire U.S. society is converted to one or the other of the three non-Advocate Worldview structures. That is, it will continue unless Advocates step forward and say in unison, 'This just should not be!'" and then they place into office people that hold to the Advocate's Worldview.

*All that is needed for Evil to succeed
is for Good men to do nothing.*

One Last Example: The Tax Structure of the United States. To illustrate the change that has occurred in the structure of society in the United States, consider the tax structure that is now in place. This is perhaps the most dramatic of the features that have changed. The tax structure reflects the non-Advocate Worldview solution of those who were in control of society. The change in the tax structure has given government the ability to control most of the individual's activities – your activities. There is synergy between these two features: the tax code laws, and Government's ability to control your activities. The synergy between the two has resulted in a tax code that has become, in size and reach, unbearably intrusive in the lives of individual Americans. That synergy is still causing the code to grow, and its intrusiveness continues to grow. The desire for control has not only been cast over individuals in society, it has been cast over every group, every organization, and every business enterprise. The tax structure in the United States has become a giant and powerful tool that government uses with impunity to control society. The Income Tax laws, which are only a part of the total tax structure, have resulted in individuals being sent to jail for no other reason than non-conformance with the government created tax code.

The tax code's control is aimed at the average American. The intrusion just begins with control over your income. While everyone tries to avoid this fact, it is true none-the-less: The tax structure is implemented from the point of view that the proceeds of your labor belongs to the government. It doesn't matter how you earned it or what expense and effort you put in to creating the income, it is not yours. The government is being generous in letting you keep some of it. Even criminals, if they kept all that they received from their illegal enterprise and did not keep only that portion that the government allowed them to keep, they go to jail for failing to acknowledge government's ownership of the benefits received from their labor. It doesn't matter to the government that the criminal is never convicted of their other crimes. Under the current tax structure, crime is viewed by the government as a civil matter, not a governmental matter. The reach of the tax structure continues to expand every time the government perceives a new 'need': religious organizations, gun ownership, business activities, health care, politics, education, . . . There is no limit to the government's intrusive reach over the lives of individuals using this feature of society.

"No nation is permitted to live in ignorance with impunity."[31]

As the Worldview structure implemented caused the creation of this confiscatory tax structure, it also caused another feature of society to disappear. The federal government used to get the bulk of its revenue from an across the board tariff on imported goods. Insuring the security and continuous flow of imports of goods, services and raw materials that citizens and companies in the US wanted to buy was the government's job. It was a characteristic of the federal government. The government was responsible to see to it that imports occurred. As the government performed this service to its citizens, it earned revenue. When individuals pursuing the Enforcer's, Defender's and Controller's Worldviews gained control of government, they pushed for the 16th amendment to the US Constitution. The 16th amendment allows the government to take your earnings. Despite the fact that this amendment to the constitution was declared unconstitutional by the Supreme Court of the United States[32], nevertheless, it was implemented and from that time on, with the arrival of their new found powers, those in control of the US government shifted the government's focus to the confiscation of the bulk of its revenue by just taking earnings – yours, theirs, businesses, criminals – whose earnings does not matter. If someone has income, they were to send the government everything except that portion the government determined they could keep. Of course, government chose to hide the actual severity of the tribute they were demanding by merely disguising the offering with the label of an income tax – a modest amount of your total earnings that they will determine and that everyone has the responsibility to pay. The principle is the same – pay the extortion fee immediately on the benefits you received from your labor or you will lose your rights to live here as a 'free' person. The income tax structure sets the hierarchy in our society. It is clear who works for whom.

The government abandoned its responsibilities to international commerce because it did not need the revenue from the tariff imposed on imported goods. The feature of the services provided by the government disappeared as those in control pursued the enormous controlling power they had gained over your decisions and those of every business in the country. Think about how your life would change if there were no income tax today. Everything you earned would be yours to spend or save as you liked. Today the government effectively dictates how much of what you earn is yours to keep. They control how much you save, for what purposes, when you can withdraw the money for use, even how much the banks will give to you as interest. When the government wants, it can create special tax brakes, special fines, perform extensive audits that will cripple any business, make normal business transactions illegal . . . the list of controls that the government can create and has created is close to endless.

Consider all of the features in society that have been created and have changed since income tax was implemented: Consider all the characteristics of features of society that would change again if the income tax features were to be eliminated from society. Features exists in society because they were created to accommodate the needs of the non-Advocate's Worldviews. The entire tax structure today is a non-Advocate tax structure. An Advocate's Worldview tax structure would have a tax collected at the point of sale and transfer of tangible goods, collected by local governments, and passed sequentially to the other levels of government. A few of the advantages to this tax structure would include the ability of local governments to insure that services are not duplicated; local governments would have better control over the spending habits of county, state, and federal governments; and, local governments would be more receptive to commerce occurring in their communities because commerce is where they would obtain their revenue instead of confiscatory real estate taxes. Additionally, you would own the proceeds of your labor until you decided to spend the proceeds and there would be no penalties for saving your money and withdrawing it no matter where you saved it or why you withdrew it. Of course, with the Advocate's Worldview tax structure the government would lose the controls it has over society and your life, which is the whole point.

The future of society is in your hands. If you understand The Political Teachings of Jesus Christ, and Thomas Payne's Common Sense essays, you will also understand exactly what has changed over the years in the structure and features of United State's society. If you pick up and read Lindburg's book and Thomas Payne's essays, and reflect on what you have read in this Political Primer, you will know what you have to do if you want to reestablish the original Worldview principles upon which our country was founded.

WARNING!

Is the structure of society today 'just not right?
Get politically active!
Do you like the way society is currently being structured?
Get politically active!
People whose Reality 'just should not be'
are demonstrating in streets!

A Parting Thought.

You have heard this question many times,
"What is mightier than the sword?"

And of course the answer you have always heard is,
"The pen."

But have you ever been asked,
"What is mightier than the pen?"
The answer is:
A personal commitment!

Make a commitment,
Register with and support the political party that is pursuing your Worldview.
The structure of the society you live in is at stake!

Appendix A

THE HE/SHE DILEMMA

Gender has been a problem for writers ever since it became important to be 'politically correct'. A brief discussion on gender can be found in "Publication Manual of the American Psychological Association. This author has abandoned the grammatically correct but awkward and annoying sentence construction using 'he or she', 'him or her', he/she, etc., or the alternate use of the singular pronouns he and then she. To achieve gender neutrality, the author has adopted the vocal practice of using 'they' or 'them' or 'themself' to reference the fact that only one he or only one she or many he's and/or she's are being referenced. The number can always be determined by looking at the context of the sentence, the verb, and whether a singular suffix such as 'self' was used.

To the extent that this practice offends people, the author apologizes and suggests that you consider the advantages. Haven't you heard, especially in heated conversations, people ask, "Who are 'they'?" "Who are the "they" that you are referring to?" Well, who do you think the "they" are? Consider this statement:

An individual doesn't say 'he or she' when they are talking. They say 'they' when they mean 'he or she'.

Now consider the more grammatically correct alternative structure to this statement.

An individual doesn't say 'he or she' when he or she is talking, he or she will say 'they' when he or she means 'he or she'.

Mark E. Glogowski, Ph.D.

Which sentence structure is easier to read? The use of 'they' refers to nothing more than either a collection of many he's and she's or just one individual that could be a he or a she.

Also, the author believes in the principle of 'Nutes and Naughts', i.e., if an individual takes a position with power or status, the individual should take the title that goes with that position. For example, if the position of control over a group is "Chairman", women lose, at the very least, a modicum of prestige by being called 'Chairwoman' because doing so forces people to subconsciously at least, acknowledge that special consideration of some sort has been granted to the person because the person is a female. To be called an inanimate object, a 'Chair', is tantamount to being a object that doesn't move and that people sit on. It is better to be called "Madam Chairman" – preserving the title that historically unquestionably has authority, yet still shows respect for the person as a female.

The principle of Nutes and Naughts was first revealed to the author by Michael Long during a Toastmasters International speech contest in 1985. He discussed women's feeble attempt to eliminate masculine endings and noted that "Chairwoman" still ends in "...man". Human, a generic term that includes women still ends in "..man". The principle of Nutes and Naughts suggests titles never be changed to be politically (or sexually) correct.

Appendix B

POLITICS CAN BECOME VERY COMPLEX VERY QUICKLY

Using the concepts of Worldviews and PU statements, the following will illustrate how ignoring these two fundamental concepts can quickly result in total political confusion.

Only if you let it! Some people hold the opinion that

Politics is too complex to be boiled down into just four 'Worldviews'. After all, it is next to impossible to get just two people to agree on some things, and they certainly don't agree on everything like The Political Primer would suggest. If you throw a third person into the mix, total agreement on every issue is – well – it is just impossible!

The opinion just expressed could not be further from the truth. Sure, it is often difficult to get political agreement when people meet. But, the approach to politics described in *The Political Primer* is not just a theory. When you put the teachings of *The Political Primer* into practice, a lot of what you observe on the political scene is easily explained. So, while politics may appear to be complex and confusing, it will stay that way only if you let it. How complex? Take a look.

Determining the complexity. In the past, while there was no way to calculate quantitatively how complex our perception of politics was, now thanks to the political concepts provided in Part 1, we can perform this analysis. This fairly long but straightforward analysis illustrates why politics is perceived to be complex. To start, assume two people are meeting to talk about one single issue. Assume also that neither individual knows what their personal political Worldview is. Also assume they do not

Mark E. Glogowski, Ph.D.

know what the other individual's Worldview is. This is not much of an assumption since most people today do not know what their Worldview is and they don't know what other people's Worldviews are. This fact is reflected in the fact that most politicians will not discuss their Worldviews – because they don't know what their Worldview is. To make matters even more confusing, many of the politicians that know what their Worldview is have deliberately joined the wrong party.

That makes our assumptions pretty much equivalent to you turning on television to watch a political debate between two politicians. How many potential combinations of political beliefs and biases does the debate represent?

What is a constant in this analysis is that each individual will bring only one opinion into the discussion. So, the analysis need only deal with one opinion per individual. That opinion is formed from a combination of the individual's Worldview and their PU statement induced bias beliefs. Since each individual brings only one opinion into the debate, the two individuals will represent only one possible combination of two potential political opinions. The question we will determine here is:

How many potential combinations of political opinions are there that can exist of which these two people will represent only one of?

What would you guess? Two? Three? Ten? Fifty? Can there possibly be that many combinations of political opinion when only two people are present?

Two Factors Determine the Complexity of Politics. Two factors will influence the political opinions brought into a conversation on an issue by the two individuals. The first factor, and perhaps most important, is whether the two people in question share the same Worldview. The second is whether either of the two individuals, or both, were impacted by a PU statement.

Political Opinion = Worldview + PU Statement induced bias

In the next several paragraphs we will examine these two factors and look at the different permutations (combinations) of opinions (Worldview plus bias) that could initially exist when two people meet. The scenario (situation) first considered will be the simplest, that is, where the two people are not impacted by a PU statement and they hold the same political Worldview (Table 1). Next the scenarios will consider the two individuals holding the same Worldview but impacted by a successful PU statement. After reviewing these combinations of political beliefs and biases, the scenarios where the two individuals do not share Worldviews will be reviewed, followed by an analysis of the impact of the PU statements when the two individuals do not share Worldviews. As you proceed through this analysis, keep in mind that if the two individuals are picked at random, the combination of political beliefs and biases observed will be one of the combinations illustrated in the analysis below, but only one! Your job, as a voter, is to determine what the candidates Worldview is and separate their Worldview from their biases and then choose a candidate that shares your Worldview. How difficult can that be?

Both Individuals Have the Same Worldview. For this evaluation consider two people, A and B, where each person is unaware of their own personal Worldview and neither person knows what the Worldview of the other person is. The Political Primer teaches that if two people share the same Worldview, they share the same political beliefs and they will agree with each other concerning the Direction and Approach to any solution. This is the ideal situation because each of the individual's biases will be that of their political Worldview. Illustrated in Table 1 is the number of permutations of political opinions that can exist when two people share the same Worldview. Because the Worldview being shared is unknown, the shared Worldview can be any one of four possible combinations. One of these combinations of opinions is the combination you are looking for when you select your candidate(s) to support. All you have to do is to figure out which Worldview you hold. The candidate that holds your Worldview is the candidate you should support.

Table 1
Both individuals have the same Worldview.
Neither individual (A nor B) were influenced by a PU statement.

Table 1
Both individuals have the same Worldview.
Neither individual (A nor B) were influenced by a PU statement.

	Worldview 1	Worldview 2	Worldview 3	Worldview 4
Combination 1	AB			
Combination 2		AB		
Combination 3			AB	
Combination 4				AB

In this table, and in the tables that follow, A and B represent the personal Worldviews of the two individuals.

Same Worldview, Both Individuals Identically Impacted by a PU Statement. Consider the impact of a PU statement. Keep in mind that the successful PU statements causes the individual to suppress their Worldview for at least one issue and causes the individual to adopt a solution which is contrary to the individual's Worldview. That solution becomes a personal political bias of the individual because the solution is created from a Worldview other than from the Worldview held by the individual. If this happens, the number of combinations of political opinions (beliefs and biases) will increase. In Table 2 is shown the combinations of political opinions that can arise when both individuals have the same Worldviews and then chose to support the same biased solution. There are twelve combinations of political beliefs and biases that meet the conditions in this scenario. In Table 2, the letters $\underline{A}$ and $\underline{B}$ still represent the personal Worldview of the two individuals, and $\underline{a}$ and $\underline{b}$, respectively, represent the biased solution that was embraced because of a PU statement. When listening to a political discussion or debate you will interpret the PU statement biased **ab** views as an indication that the individuals hold the indicated Worldview that **ab** was listed under. While they are discussing the issue you will have no indication from the discussion that they actually hold the Worldview **AB** was listed under. Their discussion would lead you to the conclusion that the individual held the Worldview of their expressed bias, listed as ab. This can only lead to political confusion.

Table 2
Both individuals have the same Worldview.
Both were identically influenced by a PU statement

	Worldview 1	Worldview 2	Worldview 3	Worldview 4
Combination 5	AB	ab		
Combination 6	AB		ab	
Combination 7	AB			ab
Combination 8	ab	AB		
Combination 9		AB	ab	
Combination 10		AB		ab
Combination 11	ab		AB	
Combination 12		ab	AB	
Combination 13			AB	ab
Combination 14	ab			AB
Combination 15		ab		AB
Combination 16			ab	AB

Notice in Table 2 the absence of 'ab' (the political bias) in the same cell as AB (Worldview). If the solution embraced by the two individuals as a bias is the same solution that would have resulted from the individuals' Worldview, the combinations of political opinion would be identical to those shown in Table 1. There are consequences to the individual when the individual adopts a solution as a bias rather than arriving at that same solution by logically deriving the solution from their Worldview: The bias creates a prejudicial impoundment of the individual's political principles, which is not a good situation for the individual because the bias will result in irrational discussions – discussions based on emotions rather than beliefs. (This is a topic for another day.)

With 12 possible combinations of political beliefs and bias, the potential number of combinations of political opinions, from which only one combination could be present, has now climbed to 16.

Mark E. Glogowski, Ph.D.

Same Worldview, but Only One Person Impacted by PU Statement. If only one person was impacted by a PU statement and the other is was not, and you did not know which person was influenced, the result is the creation of another 24 more combinations of possible political opinions that could exist. These are depicted in Table 3.

Table 3
Both individual have the same Worldview.
Only one person was influenced by a PU statement.

	Worldview 1	Worldview 2	Worldview 3	Worldview 4
Combination 17	AB	a		
Combination 18	AB		a	
Combination 19	AB			a
Combination 20	AB	b		
Combination 21	AB		b	
Combination 22	AB			b
Combination 23	a	AB		
Combination 24		AB	a	
Combination 25		AB		a
Combination 26	b	AB		
Combination 27		AB	b	
Combination 28		AB		b
Combination 29	a		AB	
Combination 30		a	AB	
Combination 31			AB	a
Combination 32	b		AB	
Combination 33		b	AB	
Combination 34			AB	b
Combination 35	a			AB
Combination 36		a		AB
Combination 37			a	AB
Combination 38	b			AB
Combination 39		b		AB
Combination 40			b	AB

The total potential combinations of political opinions that can now be accounted for, of which only one could be present when two people meet, has increased to 40.

The number of political opinions that can be present is getting quite large.

Same Worldview, and Both Individuals Impacted Differently by a PU Statement. Consider the scenarios where the individuals share the same Worldview but after being exposed to PU statements both were impacted differently by the PU statements and the individuals embraced different solutions derived from different Worldviews. This would cause the number of possible combinations of political opinions to increase by another 24 possible different combinations. These scenarios are shown in Table 4.

Mark E. Glogowski, Ph.D.

Table 4
Both individuals have the same Worldview.
Each individual was influenced differently by PU statement.

	Worldview 1	Worldview 2	Worldview 3	Worldview 4
Combination 41	AB	a	b	
Combination 42	AB	a		b
Combination 43	AB	b	a	
Combination 44	AB		a	b
Combination 45	AB	b		a
Combination 46	AB		b	a
Combination 47	a	AB	b	
Combination 48	a	AB		b
Combination 49	b	AB	a	
Combination 50		AB	a	b
Combination 51	b	AB		a
Combination 52		AB	b	a
Combination 53	a	b	AB	
Combination 54	a		AB	b
Combination 55	b	a	AB	
Combination 56		a	AB	b
Combination 57	b		AB	a
Combination 58		b	AB	a
Combination 59	a	b		AB
Combination 60	a		b	AB
Combination 61	b	a		AB
Combination 62		a	b	AB
Combination 63	b		a	AB
Combination 64		b	a	AB

The total number of combinations of political opinions, of which only one will be present, increases to 64. That's sixty four different potential combinations of political opinions on one topic that can be created when two people meet and they share <u>the same Worldview</u>. No wonder people believe politics is complex.

The complexity is becoming pretty bad... **Different Worldviews.** Consider now the scenarios where the two people do not share the same Worldview, such as in a debate, and neither person has been impacted by a PU statement. In Table 1, when both A and B shared the same Worldviews there were just four possible combinations of political beliefs that could be represented when they met. If they do not hold the same Worldview, which is most likely the case, and are unaffected by PU statements, there can be as many as 12 combinations of political opinions. These twelve combinations are shown in Table 5.

Table 5
Each individual has a different Worldview.
Neither individual was influenced by a PU statement.

	Worldview 1	Worldview 2	Worldview 3	Worldview 4
Combination 65	A	B		
Combination 66	A		B	
Combination 67	A			B
Combination 68	B	A		
Combination 69		A	B	
Combination 70		A		B
Combination 71	B		A	
Combination 72		B	A	
Combination 73			A	B
Combination 74	B			A
Combination 75		B		A
Combination 76			B	A

The number of combinations of political opinions that have been identified as potentially being represented by two individuals meeting has now increased to 76.

But, this is worse... **Different Worldviews, Both Identically Impacted by a PU Statement.** In Table 5 is displayed the twelve different combinations of Worldviews that could exist when two people do not hold the same Worldview. Now consider the scenario where the two individuals do not share the same Worldview and after being impacted by PU statements both support the <u>same</u> solution where that solution was not derived from either person's Worldviews. This scenario, the combinations of which is shown in Table 6, increases to 100 the number of potential combinations of

Mark E. Glogowski, Ph.D.

political opinions from which two individuals meeting to discuss one issue would represent just one combination thereof.

Table 6
Each individual has a different Worldview.
Both individuals were influenced identically by a PU statement.

	Worldview 1	Worldview 2	Worldview 3	Worldview 4
Combination 77	A	B	ab	
Combination 78	A	B		ab
Combination 79	A	ab	B	
Combination 80	A		B	ab
Combination 81	A	ab		B
Combination 82	A		ab	B
Combination 83	B	A	ab	
Combination 84	B	A		ab
Combination 85	ab	A	B	
Combination 86		A	B	ab
Combination 87	ab	A		B
Combination 88		A	ab	B
Combination 89	B	ab	A	
Combination 90	B		A	ab
Combination 91	ab	B	A	
Combination 92		B	A	ab
Combination 93	ab		A	B
Combination 94		ab	A	B
Combination 95	B	ab		A
Combination 96	B		ab	A
Combination 97	ab	B		A
Combination 98		B	ab	A
Combination 99	ab		B	A
Combination 100		ab	B	A

And Worse...

Different Worldviews, One Individual Impacted by a PU Statement. The potential number of variations of political beliefs and biases possible when both individuals hold different Worldviews and only one of them was impacted by a PU statement is only partially illustrated in Table 7 because just one variation of the twelve combinations of Worldviews from Table 5 was used to illustrate the possibilities. When all twelve possible variations of the combinations of the two Worldviews are considered, Table 7 represents just six of a total of 72 different unique combinations of political opinions when two people meet and do not share the same Worldview and one of them was impacted by a PU statement.

Table 7
Each individual has a different Worldview
Only one individual was influenced by a PU statement

	Worldview 1	Worldview 2	Worldview 3	Worldview 4
Combination 101	A	Ba		
Combination 102	A	B	a	
Combination 103	A	B		a
Combination 104	Ab	B		
Combination 105	A	B	b	
Combination 106	A	B		b

The total number of potential combinations of political opinions (Worldviews plus biases) is now 172.

And worse... **Different Worldview and Differently Impacted by a PU Statement.** Finally, the last scenario to be considered is where both individuals hold different Worldviews and both were impacted differently by a PU statement, and they now support different biased solutions for the issue under discussion. Illustrated in Table 8 are nine possible combinations of political opinion that can occur for just one combination of Worldviews shown in Table 5. Table 8 therefore represents an additional 108 combinations of political opinions.

Mark E. Glogowski, Ph.D.

Table 8
Each individual has a different Worldview
Both individuals were influenced differently by a PU statement.

	Worldview 1	Worldview 2	Worldview 3	Worldview 4
Combination 173	Ab	Ba		
Combination 174	Ab	B	a	
Combination 175	Ab	B		a
Combination 176	A	Ba	b	
Combination 177	A	B	ba	
Combination 178	A	B	b	a
Combination 179	A	Ba		b
Combination 180	A	B	a	b
Combination 181	A	B		ab

This brings the total number of combinations of political opinions accounted for to 280. Two people meeting to discuss one issue would be just one combination of the 280 combinations so far identified. That's 280 different possible combinations of political opinions (beliefs and biases) that could be represented on just one issue. Can you as an independent observer truly believe you can figure out the political Worldviews and PU induced biases the two individuals based on their responses to a few questions about a single issue? For any third party observer (which you are) it is very difficult to determine a person's political Worldview versus their political biases when you have no control over the questions being asked. If you have no clue what your Worldview is or how it impacts your political beliefs, you have just scratched the surface of the problem. The number of potential combinations of political opinions increases dramatically when a third person, you, are accounted for in the anaylsis.

No wonder people seem confused.

Add a Third Person to the Mix. When a third person enters a discussion, if the third person had not been influenced by a PU statement, the number of potential combinations of political opinions that are possible (of which the three individuals will represent only one combination) jumps to 1,220. If the third person comes in with a PU influenced bias concerning the issue at hand, the potential combination of political opinions jumps to a whopping 4,880! That's four thousand eight hundred and eighty different possible combinations of political opinions (Worldviews and PU induced biases) on just one issue. The three individuals involved, the two debators and yourself, will only represent one of those combinations of political opinions. If you listen to another set of three people discussing the same issue, you have a good chance of having only had the benefit of hearing two potential sets of opinions out of the 4,880 that exist.

Politics is just insane. Can't anyone just get along?

The Problem with the Complexity. Let's assume you are able to figure out which combination of political opinion was being represented by the two (or three) individuals in the debates. How do you figure out which part of their opinion is based on their Worldview and which part is based on bias that was instilled by a PU statement? How do you determine if any of the individuals share your Worldview? If you liked what they said, was it because they agreed with your Worldview, or was it because they said something that agrees with your PU statement induced bias on the subject?

The answers to the Political Interrogatories will help you sort out this mess. Politics is really not that complicated if you don't let it be.

Glossary

Advocate: A person that advocates a Liberal Republican Worldview

Approach: The choice between creating laws that empower individuals because they are Good versus laws that restrain individuals because they are Evil.

Change: Placing individuals in control of society that will pursue a different Worldview than the one being pursued by those in government.

Characteristics: The aspects of Features of Society that can change.

conservative: Used fiscally to reference a person that is modest and reserved in actions and desires.

Conservative: A person that believes people are basically and inherently Evil.

Controller: A person that advocates a Conservative Republican Worldview

Defender: A person that advocates a Liberal Democrat Worldview

Democrat: A person that believes the government is responsible for the welfare of the individual.

Direction: The choice between the individual or the government being empowered to make the decisions related to the individual's welfare.

Enforcer: A person that advocates a Conservative Democrat Worldview

Evil: The inherent motivation of other people being to hurt you or to not care if their actions harm you.

Expectation: Your anticipation of another individual displaying either Good or Evil characteristics; Your prediction of how pending interactions with other people will most likely end.

Mark E. Glogowski, Ph.D.

Feature of Society: Tangible elements of society, such as laws, people, services, organizations, customs, merchandise, businesses, etc.: Any aspect of society that can be labeled, counted, used, analyzed, or manipulated is a feature of society.

Good: The inherent motivation of other people being to help you.

Liberal: A person that believes people are basically and inherently Good.

Mantras: Statements continuously repeated; the political intent is to arouse emotions in the targeted individual.

Moderate: A person that verbally advocates one Worldview but pursues a different Worldview.

PAC Factor: Political Awareness Confusion Factor: A measure of your political awareness and political confusion.

Political Beliefs: The sum of your Worldview plus your political biases.

Political Bias: A belief or political position on an issue that you began to support after you were subjected to a PU Statement; your political bias may or may not be consistent with your Worldview.

Problem: The existence of undesirable shifts in the characteristics of features of society.

PU Statement: A political untruth or a politically unrelated statement.

Reality: A conclusion concerning what you believe about how the world does work as determined by your Expectation and your concept of Responsibility.

reality: What you observe to be real and have no ability to determine or control.

Republican: A person that believes the individual is responsible for their own welfare.

Responsibility: Your conclusion concerning whether you or other people (a governing authority) should make decisions on issues that impact you.

responsibility: The acceptance of the consequences of a decision being made and implemented.[Note: the following distinction applies to the terms "Responsibility" and "responsibility":

When "Responsibility" is used, it is a reference to the conclusion you made concerning who should and will make the decisions during the decision making process; when "responsibility" is used it invariably refers to the consequences after the implementation of the decision.]

Societal Structure: The immediate configuration and association of society around an individual (business, common, poor, criminal, elite, etc.).

Solution: The creation of series of steps for people to take that will reduce or eliminate undesirable characteristics of features of society.

Structure of Society: The guiding principle of the Worldview that is being followed and used to create solutions to society's problems comprised of a Worldview's Direction and Approach.

The Political Gap: The difference between your Reality and your Worldview

Themself: A substitute for "Himself or herself", "him or her self", or "himself/herself", etc., and similar variations.

Worldview: What you believe about how the world should work. Worldviews are the basis of all political philosophies and are identified by the two Political Interrogatories.

ENDNOTES

Note from the Author

1. Politics for Dummies, Ann DeLaney, 1995, IDG Books Worldwide, Inc, New York, NY
2. To minimize the influence of 'what other people think' and keep to keep the focus on the fundamental political concepts and how they affect the reader's beliefs, this Political Primer will cite very few references.
3. Magic Eye®, visit www.magiceye.com for more information. Magic Eye, Inc. Provincetown, MA.

Chapter 1. Politics – It is All About You

4. See Appendix B, The He/She Dilemma; See also <u>Publication Manual of the American Psychological Association</u>, Fifth Edition, 2001, Washington DC, pg 66.
5. <u>I'm OK. You're OK, A Practical Guide to Transactional Analysis,</u> Thomas A. Harris, M.D., 1969, Harper & Row, Publishers, Inc., New York. Note: If you haven't read Dr Harris's book, it is suggested you do so <u>after</u> reading this Political Primer. If you have read Dr Harris's book, read it again after finishing this political primer and the text will have a much different, and perhaps clearer meaning

Chapter 2. Six Fundamental Political Concepts

6. Dr Harris' theory has been used to explain the existence of the criminal element of society: If the individual's Reality is that they are 'not OK' and basically Evil, and that other people are also not OK and basically Evil, such individuals have no concern about what they do. No matter what they do it will be wrong. Their attitude is that if anyone is going to benefit from a decision, then they are going to make the decision. And, if

people are harmed by their decision, oh well, so what? Let the chips fall where they fall. People get what they deserve!

Chapter 3. Politics is War

7   Quinn and Rose, Broadcast station WSAY, 1040 AM, Canandaigua, NY
8   <u>Guilty</u>, Ann Coulter, 2008, Random House, New York
9   Mantras are sacred utterances deliberately invoking divinity during prayer. They are also believed to possess magical powers during incantations. In politics, a mantra is a statement continuously repeated with the intent of arousing emotions in the targeted voter.
10 As one of perhaps hundreds of examples that could be cited, take the case of Roger Rohrbach, Rochester, New York. Mr Rohrbach was an elected Democrat official. Redistricting caused his district and those of his Democratic colleagues to be changed. The Democrats found themselves with too many incumbant candidates and too few districts to run them in. Mr Rohrbach, having failed to be chosen by the Democratic party, was quickly endorsed by the Republican Party to run on the Republican Party's line. Rohrbach stated that he was a Democrat, believes in the Democratic party's philosophy, and will always vote with the Democrats. The Republican Party's committee nominated him anyway and placed him on the ballot as a Republican "because he can win". The reader is referred to the essays in Part 3: 'What it means to be a Moderate' and 'Party Jumper'
11 Bruce Williams, "My World", WHAM, Rochester, NY, June 26, 2000. ~9:00 AM
12 How to Make Cold Calls,

Chapter 5 Classify Yourself

13 The Author's Worldview shows through here because any other Worldview would have resulted in a different wording for this sentence. For example, this sentence could have been worded, '… you would decide quickly, going into every interaction, whether you would be given Responsibility and authority …"

Chapter 7. Four New Political Terms

14 Government can not be Responsible for an individual obeying the law. Perhaps this is why, when Democrats are asked the First Political Interrogatory, they have difficulty with the question and sort of stare blankly as if you just said something stupid. They never think of citizens being responsible for themself. They only associate the term responsible with 'responsibility to obey the law'. Republicans typically spontaneously blurt out their answer – "The Individual!"

15 Guidelines are laws, rules, regulations, codes, policies, practices, customs, standards, conditions and procedures that affect an individual's or group's actions or decisions.

16 This is a rewording of the Serenity Prayer, which was originally written by theologian Reinhold Niebuhr in the 1930's or 40's as part of a sermon. Though the full prayer is longer, the Serenity Prayer is best known for the first three lines: "God grant me serenity to accept the things I cannot change, courage to change the things I can, and wisdom to know the difference." The complete prayer is *"God, grant me the serenity to accept the things I cannot change, Courage to change the things I can, and the wisdom to know the difference. Living one day at a time; Enjoying one moment at a time; Accepting hardship as the pathway to peace. Taking, as He did, this sinful world as it is, not as I would have it. Trusting that He will make all things right if I surrender to His Will; That I may be reasonably happy in this life, and supremely happy with Him forever in the next. Amen"*

Chapter 11. Creating the Structure of Society

17 Patrick Henry. **"Give me Liberty, or give me Death!"** is a famous quotation attributed to <u>Patrick Henry</u> from a speech he made to the <u>Virginia Convention</u>. It was given on March 23, 1775, at <u>St. John's Church</u> in <u>Richmond, Virginia</u>. The quote was actually the last part of Mr Henry's speech, which is reported to end with, "...Why stand we here idle? What is it that gentlemen wish? What would they have? Is life so dear, or peace so sweet, as to be purchased at the price of chains and slavery? Forbid it, Almighty God! I know not what course others may take; but as for me, give me liberty or give me

death!" [Extracted from Wikpedia]; See also: The Worldvook Encyclopedia, Volume 9, pg 189, World Book, Inc., Chicago, IL, 2010.

18 General John Stark. **"Live Free or Die"** the official motto of the State of <u>New Hampshire</u>, adopted by the state in 1945, was part of a toast by General John Stark on July 31, 1809 sent by letter to the attendants of an anniversary reunion of the Battle of Bennington. His toast was "Live free or die: Death is not the worst of evils" [Extracted from Wikpedia.]; See also: The New Hampsire Almanac: State Emblem on the New Hampshire government website, www.nh.gov and references therein.

Chapter 13. The Homeless

19 The policy of The Mercy House in Rochester, NY, run by the Sister's of Mercy, is to provide aid and assistance to anyone that comes through the door and asks for help. The facility is operated entirely on private donations, and refuses to accept any form of government assistance.

Chapter 18. Abortion

20 Slander, by Ann Coulter, 2007,
21 Democrat and Chronical, January 22, 2011, pg 13A, "Redefine the recognition of life".

Chapter 27. Beware the Party Jumper

22 McCarthyism references an episode in American history where a senator was duped by Congress. This is a description of what happened using a totally non-related, fictitious scenario to make the events that occurred easier to understand.

Consider a task where your job is to investigate a truckload of writing instruments. You must determine if any of the writing instruments are pencils. The process of checking writing instruments required that standards be set and each writing instrument meet those standards; for example, specifically, 1) the writing instrument must contain no 'lead' center (actually a carbon black center) and 2) they must contain some form of ink to function. You are told you will be given a selection from the truckload of writing instruments and that selection will be writing instruments that are suspected pencils. If you found a pencil you could then investigate the entire truckload of writing instruments. If you did not find a pencil, the assumption would be that there are no pencils in the truckload. You are then given a group of writing instruments, pre-selected to insure all were pens and none were pencils. You found no pencils. Your conclusion, based on the criteria you were given, is that if these were the suspected pencils, then there are no pencils in the entire truckload.

McCarthyism was not about weeding out the lead pencils. It was about weeding out Communists from the US government and its agencies. Joseph McCarthy was given essentially the same instructions. Joe McCarthy was a U.S. Senator charged with investigating the political background of a number of people selected by the Democratically controlled congress and were labeled as suspected Communists. They were all cleared. None were determined to be Communists, but the individuals' lives were politically over. The investigation was labeled a witch hunt, which it was. The claim that resulted was that there were no communists in the US government or any of its agencies, which McCarthy theoretically proved using the flawed process he was tied to. Truth is, there were Communists in the government and its agencies: The American people were deceived[2].

Slander, Ann Coulter, 2003, Crown Publishing Group, NY, NY.

Chapter 29. Judges

MONROE BAR KNOCKS JUDICIAL HOPEFUL, Rochester Democrat and Chronicle, Thursday, May 19, 2011, Michael Seigler, Staff writer.

The Livingston County District Attorney was reviewed as a candidate by the Monroe County Bar Association but failed to be interviewed. He was given a rating of 'not qualified.' The lawyers in Monroe County that conducted the review were claimed to have had little, or no contact with the individual on a professional level – but that did not give them cause to excuse themselves from providing input to the evaluation process.

The president of the association insisted the rating was not based on the candidate's decision to not be interviewed by the association, and that the association made the decision based on the other available information. According to the article, the committee evaluated candidates based on Experience, Legal analysis, Judicial temperament and Demeanor, Sensitivity to Discrimination, Ethics and Integrity, and Communication skills. The Livingston County Bar Association unanimously endorsed the District Attorney as qualified. If both bar associations reviewed the same information, should they not have been in agreement? Obviously the reviewer's Worldviews played a role in their decision.

[25] See footnote in Chapter 1 and Appendix A

Chapter 31

[26] A controversy is currently brewing over the violence at the border with Mexico. Thousands of people have died. When three ATF agents were the victim of the gun traffic into Mexico, it was revealed that the U.S. government was allowing weapons to enter Mexico unchecked. Thousands of them! The policies of the US government created the conditions and provided the means for the escalation of violence. The US government deliberately allowed the violence to escalate and ignored the increased violence perpetrated on the citizens it was suppose to protect, until that is, the recipients of the government's lax and loquacious approach to protecting its citizens backfired and instead of citizens being killed, federal ATF agents were victims of this lax enforcement of US laws.

[27] "Alabama passes 'strongest immigration bill' in U.S.", Bob Johnson, The Associated Press, June 10, 2011, Democrat and Chronicle, Front Page, Rochester, NY

Epilog

[28] In the Advocate's world, methods to enforce Expectations that seem ineffective today would be very effective: Think of the Bobbies in England that did not carry guns until the Expectations of society changed and the conduct of individuals

in society changed. Expectations were lowered, resulting in the need for Bobbies to carry guns.

29 The Political Teachings of Jesus, Tod Lindburg, 2007, Harper Collins, NY.
30 Common Sense, Glenn Beck, 2009, Simon & Shuster, NY
31 Thomas Jefferson, 1743-1826, 3rd President of the United States, 1801-1809.
32 The World Book Encyclopedia, Volume 4 "CI-CA", pg 1014, World Book, Chicago. 2010